The Live Science
of Mechanics
or of
the Machine

*

Traumear

Esoteric elements of knowledge, or **esoterica**, are derived from a direct impersonation of the divine afflatus. What we can make out in terms of such knowledge would fit on the head of a pin, however the knowledge itself brings us into contact with the god of our forefathers, prior to his inception as human. This knowledge is woven to such an extent into our modern halfway perceptions, that before we can clearly and succinctly appreciate his human presence we do well to occupy ourselves with esoterica to some extent and then we will better know how and where we stand. If such knowledge is written down, then the writer is a mere tool of creative process to which he lends himself as a recording ear, as an observing eye. As soon as the writer's personality comes into its own, esoteric knowledge is replaced by knowledge proper, real and true. In terms of our contemporary humanity therefore, esoterica amount to a useful purgative to be made use of by those who wish to be on their way to knowledge true and proper.

*

The Live Science of Mechanics
or of the Machine

Mechanical is that which moves and is moved by no other power except its own.

All motion is due to gravity. Gravity is the essence of motion. Not all motion exists. Only such motion which exists can be known.

Light is shaped energy. Whatever has a cause depends directly on light. Gravity depends directly on light because of motion. Motion is the cause of gravity.

Mechanical things are objects. An object is never at rest. All objects and their behaviour are studied by the science of mechanics and the science of mechanics is in fact the totality of objects and their behaviour. The science of mechanics is an objective study.

Every science results in a body of knowledge. The body of knowledge in which the science of mechanics results is the human body. It differs from the body of a person in that it has no individual properties. The body of a person may be a body of knowledge, but it may also carry attributes of personality. The human body also differs from this or that human body in that its appearance is not visible but invisible. All objects however are visible. The science of mechanics effects the transformation of all objects into the human body. It affects universal transformation. Since humanity is the essence of being, it must be clear from the outset that objectivity, which is the being of objects, is not limited in itself, but by human understanding. But human understanding is limited only by limitation itself and not by any other thing, and therefore objectivity is its own limit. Consequently the live science of mechanics is in no need of laws, rules or principles, and therefore it does not seek any out in objects

1

and their behaviour. The explanation of objective behaviour is a matter of course, which means that it occurs in any case of objective study, and at any rate. But the explanation of objects themselves, outside of their behaviour, and the explanation of the object itself, of its reason for being what it is where and when it is, this is left to the special study of statistics which grows out of the study of mechanics. Suffice it to be said here that the science of mechanics is the study of objects and of their behaviour not for the sake of explaining what may be observed, but in order to transform those objects into the human body by means of observation. We do well to begin therefore by studying and developing our means.

*

Observation is a process. During observation the will and the intellect are congruent. They agree with each other and concur. Agreement is only possible on a common basis, and in the case of observation the will and the intellect agree on the basis of substance. Concurrence is only possible in terms, or in terms of an end, and in the case of observation the will and the intellect concur in terms of reality.

Observation, being a process, occurs both in space and in time, and never in either of these alone. Like any process it is measured. Therefore it does not make sense to measure it again. It does make sense however to measure objects. This is achieved by comparing them to each other. The measurement of objects is intentional, while the measurement of observation is automatic.

The subject is the human being. All human beings are subjectively equal. Observation can be defined as the union of the subject with the object. Since human beings are all subjectively equal, observation does not vary in any way from one human being to the next. It does vary however from one object to the next, and with every mode of objective behaviour.

There are five modes of objective behaviour; or of behaviour, since subjects do not behave. These modes are kind, sort, type, variety, and mode itself. Modes of behaviour are observed in no way differently from objects.

Every mode of behaviour depends on the way, and is influenced by it in one way or another. The way cannot be defined, but only described. It adheres to the eightfold pattern of description, as set forth in our philosophy. Whatever happens in one way or another may be observed.

Observation includes description. Therefore it does not make sense to describe observation again. It does make sense however to describe events. Whatever can be described is eternal, and each and every event may be consistently and completely described. Whatever cannot be so described is not an event. All events are impartial.

Observation must always be careful. In the event of partiality an event has not been carefully enough observed before it was described. Eventual impartiality is the test of objective observation. Objects and behaviour are not described, but depicted. All description is immediate, but depiction is not. Depiction necessitates a medium.

Observation concludes depiction. It is therefore of no use to depict observation. It is possible however, and can be useful, to depict the medium. But no medium can be objective. It is a subjective illusion. Depiction of this illusion is useful only if it serves the depiction of objects and behaviour, and never on its own account. It is therefore not given a name of its own. We differentiate however between a picture and a scheme, where the former includes the depiction of its subjective medium, while the latter does not. Both the picture and the scheme however are legitimate depictions of objects and their behaviour.

Observation may not be artificial. This means that no instruments may be used and no tools except those of the inherent human faculty. This faculty is the will. It combines, during observation, with the congruent intellect in an infinite number of ways, and each combination results in the production of an instrument or of a tool, depending on whether the will predominates or the intellect. One of the two must predominate in the case of each and every combination, since the will and the intellect are not equal, but of common origin. If the will predominates, an instrument is made by the use of the faculty of choice. If the intellect predominates, a tool is fashioned by the use of the faculty of will-power. An instrument is applied or adapted, while a tool is employed or adopted. Application and adaptation, employment and adoption are all implied by observation. Therefore it is an insane thing to use instruments and tools in order to manipulate and treat observation. It is a useful thing however to make use of tools and instruments in order to manipulate and deal with facts.

Facts are not observed, but discovered or invented. Discovered facts comprise the realm of research, whereas invented facts make up the complex of laws. The realm of research is quite distinct from any complex of laws, and this distinction is an achievement. It is quite absurd therefore to attempt to make one fit the other, which is a principal ambition of the extinct science of mechanics, as set forth by Galileo and Newton. The precise separateness of invention and discovery is a direct result of the distinct imagination, and the distinctness of the imagination is a prerequisite of man which by definition precedes all mature activity and even the possibility of mature activity. Whatever activity commences previous to the achievement of the imagination's distinctness must always undermine to a degree and undo the human being's progress to maturity and manhood. That is exactly what happens when observations are charted according to laws, as occurs in the case of all extinct science.

Observation results in invention and discovery. They are the mind and body of the human being. The entire realm of research

4

and discovered fact is in fact the body of the human being, and the whole complex of invented fact and of laws is in fact the human being's mind. It is very important now to remain always aware of the difference between the human body, which results from the science of mechanics, and the human being's body, which results from observation. The difference is most readily appreciated when we consider that both the body and the mind of the human being result from observation, and that there is no such thing as the human mind, while the human body, on the other hand, exists, as the physical thing. The human body by definition includes a human mind and can neither be conceived nor can it exist without it. The human mind however would imply by definition that such a thing could physically exist, which is an impossibility and a contradiction in terms. The human mind must always be conceived of as the thing in itself, which decidedly does not exist. It is a thing as impossible and contradictory, as unlikely and improbable, as the illimitable vacuum, as the frictionless surface, and as infinite motion. It is as imponderable a thing as mass and as absurd by definition as the mind of the human being wishes to make it when it errs. Only presume that the human mind exists, and the universe will come apart in time. Understand on the other hand that the mind of the human being exists, and your body will become a part of the universe, which is where it belongs now and where it originally was, rather than being a part of the world.

Observation is an experiment. Every human being which has a mind and a body experiments. Experimentation is the outcome of sensation for the purpose of reality and for the sake of physical reality. Not all reality is physical. But there is no such thing as mental reality. Reality itself is the kingdom. The appearance of the kingdom is mechanical. Every man in the kingdom is an automaton, which means that he is totally self-sufficient and entirely dependent upon every other man in the kingdom. Physical reality has no individual parts. Every man therefore lives entirely for every other man, and not at all for himself. Every immature man in the kingdom is a robot. This means that he is entirely mechanized, and at least to a degree, but never totally, independent. Another name for an automaton is the soul, and another name for a robot is the son of man.

Experimentation is the process of change from the robot to the automaton. This process is entirely mechanical. This also means, of course, that it may be observed from beginning to end. It is devoid of contradiction, perfectly efficient, and exists for no reason outside of itself. Consequently it may be called the object.

The subject is not real, but illusory. It is a consequence of light. It develops so as to become part of the light, or it evolves, so as to avoid the light. Subjective evolution is not at all mechanical, and it cannot be observed, but only noticed. Objective evolution, in all seriousness, is a joke. It might be considered worth studying in a science of humour. Subjective development however is potentially mechanical, and observation allows it to become objective.

Every observation of the subject's development is a mechanism. The sum total of all mechanisms is the developing subject itself. It is referred to as I. It is important to understand now that I am real, whereas the developing subject is illusory. It is also important to realize that I am not the writer of these words, but that they are mechanisms set down by the developing subject. Another name for the developing subject is the personality, and another name for the writer of these words is (anonymous).

Motion is in reality perpetual and finite. It is the essence of change. When an object moves, it changes. It is not the same to move and to be in motion. Objects can move and they may be moved, but if something is in motion it is the developing subject. If this subject is to be in motion at least one mechanism must be operating. But it is impossible that no mechanisms at all might be operating, since that would mean that the unobservable is being observed. Therefore we can safely say that the subject is always in motion.

A mechanism either operates or else it does not. If it does not, it is said to be inoperant. Operation is a process of realization. It is not the same to operate and to be in operation. A mechanism can operate, and it may be operated on. But for something to be in operation it must be objective. Operation itself, not as a process but as a concept, means the entailment of illusion. Whatever entails illusion is an equation of the world. This does not mean that it equals the world, but that it equates the world with something else. Any equation however, no matter what it equates, is numerical. And number is the appearance of shape. Every equation therefore appears to shape something, and an equation of the world appears to shape the world. We say that its appearance has this particular purpose.

An operating mechanism differs from an inoperant mechanism, and that is its only distinguishing mark. All inoperant mechanisms are alike. Operating mechanisms appear to be alike, but actually they are not. The difference between them disappears due to action and reaction.

An operating mechanism either acts or else it reacts. Whether it does one or the other does not depend upon anything germane to the mechanism, but it depends on observation. If the mechanism is observed subjectively, which is not true observation, then the mechanism reacts. If the mechanism on the other hand is observed objectively, which is proper observation, it acts. It should be added by the way that there is no such thing as true observation or real observation, since that would be a duplication of terms. But it is possible that observation is untrue, as in the case of an observant subject. And when we wish to emphasize that observation is not untrue, we say that it is proper. A subject cannot observe, but it may be observant, which means that it notices reality, and that is a ridiculous thing to do. Nevertheless it happens and must be accounted for. This happens, when it is reacted to, as by an operating mechanism.

A discussion of negative and positive matter will be appended here, in order to forestall any doubt concerning the quality of objective or observed time.

Negative matter is schematic. It relies on positive matter. The very identification of matter as positive or negative depends on the experience of time. Time is always experienced objectively. Chronological or clock time is not experienced, but felt. Eternal time is not experienced, but lived. When time is observed, it is psycho-somatic. Experienced time cannot be given another name, because it cannot be identified separately from the experience. We only know that during the experience, or while the experience went on, which is the same thing, time must have passed, and in retrospect we refer to it as experienced time. From one experience to the next however we are made forcibly conscious, be it through circumstance or by impulse, of an interval of time. This interval is open to chance and accident. But an interval of time cannot be observed, but only passed through. If it is not passed through, negative matter accumulates. This is the secret of Lot's wife. Negative matter can be used up as soon as it is noticed, and of course if it is noticed. Once it is noticed it must be identified in terms of the next experience, even if that experience has not yet begun. The only thing which we can be sure of in the case of any and every experience is that it will contain matter, even if that matter should never even become accessible. Therefore, if we wish to be absolutely certain of not being caught in the time interval following the previous experience, we must on one hand at least recognize it, so that the outcome of probable accident and chance will be fortuitous and not wasted, and on the other hand we must rely on the one common denominator of experience, interval and experience, which is the mere passage of time, to regulate our progress. The mere passage of time is the narrow gate. During the interval, accident and chance are at least probable, not only possible. The likelihood of static interference may be small, but it is definite. Recognition of the interval allows us to enter it but we cannot leave it without paying tribute to the passage of time, and if we are clever we will do so gladly. The tribute most profitable to us is the acknowledgement of mere time as a functional and totally insensible thing. We do not know then of its presence, but we remember the anticipation of its presence, and this memory gets us through. But it only does so if we are willing to forget all just as we commence the new experience. What we must be willing to forget in other words is that we have a memory, so that we may perfectly use it, and with utmost efficiency. Memory itself will trace the passage of mere time by reflecting upon it in retrospect. Of this we have neither guarantee nor foreknowledge, but only the promise of mere faith. During this crisis we are told only to believe. And that is fortuitous accident and chance become flesh. That is the word as it is heard and the light as it is seen. The retrospect reflection of bare memory feeds on mere time as it passes, and it consists of nothing else. Consequently we interpret it, for the sake of observation, as matter, since it must at least be matter, and we denote it negatively, for a fact because we intent to negate it, and as such because any connotation at all would unnecessarily inhibit or compromise our progress.

It is because of negative matter that observation can be untrue, but not true. If we observe properly, we do so necessarily in truth. False observation is no observation, and a contradiction in terms.

Motion is finite and perpetual. That is how it is observed. If it is watched, it is movement. Nothing can be in movement, but movement is static motion. An object moves. If it moves for no apparent reason, we are watching it, and there is movement. If it moves so as to stay in motion, we are merely observing it, and there is no movement. But there may be speed. For an object to be speeding it must be moving in order to stay in motion, and it must remain in motion. A moving object remains in motion by overcoming inertia and friction. It is possible however that an object overcomes inertia and friction but does not move in order to stay in motion. It other words it remains in motion, but for no apparent reason. That object is neither watched nor observed, but apprehended, and its motion is not true. Untrue motion is materially negative and must be rejected. Subsequently, not consequently, to this rejection, the object comes to rest. Rest is suspended motion. An object at rest is observed properly and for no reason. It is the act of observation.

The act of observation, which is an object at rest, is exact objectivity. This means that the mind perceives what the body undergoes. Exact objectivity is the same as perfect subjectivity. But the two are not equal. In order to become equal, which is the realization of mechanical truth, observation must become habitual. It does so by means of simple sufficient repetition. Habitual observation is the machine.

A machine is perfect motion. It may also be called the object. Every object has a quality of motion, and consequently it must also have quantity, since quality is a prerequisite of quantity; but the quality of perfection is possessed only by the machine. Now the nature of perfection is that quality and quantity have become one. Therefore we can speak of the quality, but not of the quantity of perfection, and we know that the quality of perfection is quantity itself. Therefore it is true that the machine is pure quantity.

Man is the machine. This is the same as to say that man is a god. We observe him as the machine and we love him as a god. But not every man is a machine, or perfectly objective. In order to be a man, which is to say a mature human being, it is only necessary to strive for perfection. But this is not the same as to approach an idea of perfection, which is referred to as idealism. Idealism is the attribute of youth. The attribute of maturity is realism, which is either the establishment of an idea, or the realization of the idea. The establishment of an idea is called manhood, and the realization of the idea is divine. Divinity is not a concept, but the concept. This means that a god is as divine as god, and that he differs from god in nothing. But yet a god is clearly not god. Now if there is no difference between a god and god, and if a divine thing, due to the concept, is as divine and no less divine than divinity itself, it must be true that I am god, and that I have revealed this to you so that you may write it down and understand. And you may understand by reading what is written down here.

Man is the machine. A man differs from a machine due to his power of observation. The machine observed is the object. A man differs from an object due to his power of faith. The mature man is the perfectly developed subject, which is the subject itself. A mature man differs from a subject due to his power of concentration. The immature man, or the man who is not yet mature, is the developing subject. An immature man differs from a developing subject, or from a youth, due to his power of realization. Manhood is observed animation. A man differs from an animal due to his power of creation.

These have been five facts, each preceded by the equation of an invention and a discovery. Each of the five facts is related to the previous equation, and each equation is related to every other equation, and to itself. An equation is relation in process. Each of the five facts stated in the previous paragraph is not ordinary, but special. A special fact differs from an ordinary one in that it represents the world, rather than presenting it. Therefore the world is contained in every special fact. It is also true that the five equations set down in the previous paragraph are not usual equations, but exceptional ones. The usual equation differs from the exceptional on in that it contains the universe, rather than making it available. Every exceptional equation is a key to the universe therefore, and it may be referred to as a sign. But the universe is the totality of all signs, which is equal to saying that

11

the world is the totality of all facts. Consequently we have proven that the world is the key to the universe.

This brings us to a consideration of the position of the earth. Unless we view it as part of the solar system, it does not move. In fact it is the only stationary thing in the universe. But it is not at rest. With respect to motion, something is stationary if it resists motion perfectly, and it is at rest if its motion is unlimited, which means that it is not in motion.

The earth is not at the centre of the universe, but it is that centre. That is its position. To say that it is at the centre of the universe would suggest that the universe had a centre except for the earth, which is not true. It is impossible to understand this and what follows unless we refrain from insisting on a universal picture. Such a thing cannot be. Its attempt is contrary to the very essence of universality, which is change. And how do we imagine change?

Whatever has a centre also has an inside and an outside. Consequently we speak of something within the universe, which suggests that it both is inside and participates there. Only one things is in the universe and does not participate in it, and that is the sun. therefore it is in the universe, but not within it. Since it is in the universe it must change. But it changes impartially. Viewed in itself, change is partial or impartial with respect to its purpose. Both kinds of change are purposeful, but partial change has a purpose whereas impartial change is a purpose.

The sun is the purpose of the earth. It changes impartially while the earth changes partially. The two are in purposeful relation, which means that one without the other cannot be. In unison they make up the focal point of the universe. The unique thing about a focal point is that it presents the opportunity for perspective. In order to gain that perspective, the focal point must be used.

Perspective is the efficient limit of perception. It is the useful optical illusion. Since we are part of the universe, we can view it in its entirely, but we cannot see it as such. If we wish to see it, we must do so in reflection. Those who are part of the world, of course, and therefore not part of the universe but contained by it, can neither view the universe as such nor can they see it in reflection.

Optical illusion is the reflection of the light. It is either spectral or useful. To be useful it must simply be used. To be spectral it must simply be rejected.

To use the reflection of the light means to obtain original light by means of inflection. Inflection necessitates a medium. This medium restitutes original light by reversing the reflective process in terms of the medium. But a medium always is terminal, meaning that it is not another thing, but the thing's limitation. As such it depends on nothing but the thing it limits. It differs, as a limitation, from a limit, in that the limit may be viewed distinctly, while the limitation may not be viewed, but can be seen. We recall that viewing and seeing are independent processes.

The medium by means of which we may obtain original light on the earth is the atmosphere. It does not automatically inflect reflected light, we repeat, but only if it is used for that purpose. The way of using the atmosphere as such a medium is by breathing.

For every focal point there must be a point of perspective. It is the point where the lines of vision converge. Only in the case of vision can we speak of lines in this manner, because vision is always straight, which means that it passes through a distance. There is no such thing as lines of sight, because sight is immediate.

The point of perspective corresponds to the focal point. This is so because vision corresponds to sight. But sight does not correspond to vision. Correspondence is either limited or unlimited, but it cannot be both. Unlimited correspondence implies the effect of an agent. This agent translates in the direction of the lesser member of the correspondence. The greater member supplies the agent. In the case of limited correspondence both members are of the same dimension, and an agent is neither required nor supplied.

The moon is an agent of correspondence, and it translates in the direction of the sun. The sun, the moon and the earth are in unlimited correspondence. A case of limited correspondence for example and by the way is the earth and Mars.

The earth is the greater member of this case of unlimited correspondence. It supplies the moon as an agent by means of gravity. This particular case of unlimited correspondence exists in terms of the gravitational field. The case of limited correspondence of which the earth and Mars are members, for example and by the way again, exists in terms of gravitational force.

The earth and the sun are of diverse dimension. This means that they differ in size. Size is an elementary factor. It cannot be envisioned, but only seen. Envisioned dimension is a static thing, and it must be measured even to be perceived. Seen dimension on the other hand, of size, is measured to begin with, and it is always measured. It may be measured again, but that is an idiotic endeavour. Idiocy is in fact a case of immeasurable doubt, and in consequence it remeasures and remeasures, but all to no avail.

Envisioned dimension has nothing to do with size, and it is a matter of large and small. All else being different, a large thing has nothing in common with a small thing. They are compared in terms of the envisioning act, or the vision, and they are comparable in whatever terms the vision proceeds. Vision is either determined or empty. The empty vision is the void, no matter how colourful it seems. Determined vision contributes to reality.

Sun dimension, or size, is not matter of large and small, but a case of greater and lesser. In fact it is a case of greater or lesser size. Now it is true that the sun is larger than the earth, and determined vision teaches us that. But the earth is greater than the sun. The sun does not have a larger size than the earth, and there really is no such thing as larger size, except in a manner of speaking. But the earth has the greater size of the two. This can be seen.

The size of the moon is exactly halfway between that of the earth and the sun. But since the moon is an agent of correspondence, its size must not only be seen in order to be determined, but also interpreted. This interpretation precedes the act of seeing it, and must itself be preceded by vision.

We say that vision and sight are congruent. Both of them must be determined. The focal point, which admits of a perspective of perception, and the point of perspective, which allows vision to be determined, meet as the optic image. This image is entirely perceived. There are no signs available to signal the entirety of this perception. It is complete however, when nothing remains to be perceived.

Interpretation is necessary if something inhibits perception. Such an inhibition occurs whenever the focal point and the point of perspective cannot meet because of indeterminate vision or because of undetermined sight. Both cannot happen at once, since determination must at least initiate the act of looking at something. But of course looking is not perceiving. The inhibition caused by indeterminate vision is always material. It may lie as much in the object as in the eye, since the two cannot become one until perception is uninhibited. If it lies in the object it is an error of measurement, and interpretation in this case simply means remeasuring. If it lies in the eye however it is a manifestation of bad conscience, and interpretation entails a program of study. In the case of undetermined sight, the inhibition lies either in the eye or in the perceiving subject, since the two cannot be one unless perception is pure. If it lies in the eye it is again a manifestation of bad conscience, and the same remedy is required. But if it originates in the perceptive subject it is an error of judgment, and no amount of study will remove it. Such an inhibition entails a confusion of truth and appearances. They are not judged to be independent from one another. The only possible remedy here is the act of rebirth. Of the inhibitions which lie in the eye and in the perceiving subject, the latter is by far the more serious. It is not only a case of misapplied principle, but it is an instance of abused reality. Such an error cannot be forgiven, though it is the only one of its kind.

In the case of the moon, interpretation must help establish its correct perception, but necessarily only the interpretation of the inhibition which lies in the perceiving subject. Once this inhibition is dissolved, none of the others can occur.

We have so far stated that the moon is exactly halfway in size between the earth and the sun, and that it translates in the direction of the sun, as an agent of correspondence supplied by the earth in terms of gravity, and as the third member of a case of unlimited correspondence, which in this case exists in terms of a gravitational field.

Translation is an immediate exchange of substance. When we translate an English word into a French word for example, we exchange the substance of verbal expression. When we translate one language into another, we depend on the similarity of all languages in terms of expressed substance. As we translate, we are agents of correspondence, in terms of expression and in terms of expressed substance in the two examples just given. Translation in terms of a gravitational field means an exchange of substance on the basis of a common meeting ground, which is inherent in the concept of the field, and it implies such an exchange in terms of direction and attraction, which implication resides in the attribute gravitation.

Now the terms of direction and attraction rely on each other for comprehension. Direction is limited by attraction, and attraction is limited by direction. Direction implies an object which moves. Attraction implies an object which is in motion. We recall that something can move without being in motion, such as an object at rest, but nothing can be in motion without moving. Consequently we say that something is attracted when it moves, and when and wherever it moves. We say that something is directed only if it is in motion. Now although everything in motion must also be moving, we cannot say that a directed thing is also attracted. This is so, because we are limited, or more precisely because we choose to limit ourselves, for the sake of proper observation, within the bounds of proficiency, and these bounds we will not abuse. To say that the directed thing is also attracted would at best observe mere or apparent logic, which is of no use whatsoever, and at less than best it would lead us astray. This has been amply proven wherever laboratory conduct is the only feasible contact with reality which is available, since the senses have been led astray and allowed to stray into the void.

We also know that not everything which is directed is direct. In order to be direct, the directed thing must be permitted free movement. This means that its motion must be aimed towards a goal, and that this goal must be interpreted as a purpose, and understood as the real purpose, and not as a good purpose or as the best purpose. Movement is free when its purpose makes available all possible directions and curtails none. Movement is constrained when one or more discernible directions must precede the understanding of the purpose. Something directs when it makes available a goal. The response may or may not be direct motion, which implies free movement. Whether the response is direct motion or indirect motion, which is to say whether a real purpose is given or not, depends not on the thing which directs, nor on the thing which is in response directed, directly or indirectly, but on the nature of the response itself, which is predicted by the nature of the two things interacting.

We possess enough information now for a preliminary discussion of the heavenly bodies.

All heavenly bodies together make up the system of the universe. It is uniformly constructed. It differs from all other systems in this.

The universal system of heavenly bodies has one point of reference, and that is the earth. It is comprised of the earth, of the planets, and of the stars. All heavenly bodies are in motion, except for the moon, which is at rest. All heavenly bodies move, except for the earth, which is stationary. The planets differ from the earth and from the stars, in that they alone have movement. The stars differ from the planets and from the earth, insofar as their motion is directed. Those stars whose motion is permanently directed are called suns. There is only one star in the universe whose motion is both permanently directed and also attracted. That is the sun. There are other suns, but their motion is unattracted. The moon is the only planet which has purposeful movement. Its movement is free. That is why it is at rest.

Motion is either circular or straight. Straight motion is motion through a distance, and circular motion is not through a distance. All circular motion is either round or elliptic. There is no such thing as round motion, but all circular motion which is round is called revolution. Elliptic motion does not have another name.

All heavenly bodies are either spheres or globes. The earth is the only globe. Spheres differ from the globe in that they revolve about an axis. Not all spheres revolve about the same axis. The axis of the stars is central, which cannot be pictured, and the axis of the planets is peripheral, which can be pictured. Revolution about a peripheral axis is revolution according to the circumference. Such revolution produces a trajectory. Revolution about a

18

central axis cannot be otherwise described, and it produces motion about a centre.

The universal system of heavenly bodies includes an ether. It is described as heavenly space. There is no such thing as outer space, except when we are astray in the void. This cannot always be avoided, but it must be guarded against. The only legitimate void is the one which impresses us incidentally or per chance.

All heavenly bodies, including the earth, are immersed in the ether. It is the medium. There are other media, but none of them support the heavenly bodies. The atmosphere is such another medium, and it includes the earth, the moon and the sun. Another medium is language, which communicates the word.

The written word, the gravitational field, and the universal either are all three descriptions of a medium. Only in the case of the ether is the description the same as the thing described. In the case of the gravitational field, description is logarithmic on the basis of gravity. Here the description and the thing described are analogous. In the case of the written word, description is literal. This means that the description coincides with the thing described.

All heavenly bodies except the earth travel along a path. This path is never a circle. The circle is an abstract concept, and the only one among these which cannot become concrete. Consequently we call it the abstract concept. The circle is also the only thing in the universe which must be described in order to be understood.

A path is always defined. This means that it does not come to an end. How it is defined depends upon the thing which defines it. Objects which travel along a path define it in terms of observation. The observed path continuously overcomes an end. It is said to be endless.

Among objects which travel along a path, only the heavenly bodies overcome the end of their defined path constantly. This means that they overcome it not only in time, but at the same time in space. Consequently such a path is not only observed, but it may be observed in reality.

The science of mechanics may also be called the science of the machine. The universal system of heavenly bodies is that machine. Every other machine which is built is a replica of that system.

The definition of a machine is matter in perfect motion. Only the system of heavenly bodies is a self-sufficient machine. It distributes matter evenly, and its output equals its input, while the product is real substance. The replica approaches the thing in perfection.

The universal system of heavenly bodies is an exact replica of the human mind. The human mind and the human body are the same. The earth is an exact replica of the human body, each thing can only have one exact replica. All others are to a degree involved.

The exact replica of the universal system of heavenly bodies is the distinct imagination. The distinct imagination and the physical human body are the same. The physical human body differs from the human body in that it includes the mind. The exact replica of the physical human body is the surface of the earth, which is called the terrestrial environment. Just as the physical human body includes the mind, so does the terrestrial environment include all of history. In that way if differs from the simple environment, which is the same as nature. When we wish to emphasize that the body, which is the same as the mind, is not the physical body, which includes the mind, we call it the simple human body. If we want to emphasize that the environment, which is the same as nature, is not the terrestrial environment, which includes all history, we call it the simple environment.

We understand now how the human being is the measure of all things. In comparison to fashioned things it is the pattern.

Among created things it is the model. As a born thing it is the design. Whenever a thing is the only one of its kind in the universe, it is an exact replica of an aspect of the human being. An exact replica is the replica, and it is the only thing in the universe which is as it is perceived. Therefore we may say that the replica is an exact replica of an aspect of the human being, and in fact it is an exact replica of the human soul.

The sun is the focal point of the system of heavenly bodies. The moon is that system's point of perspective. The earth is its point of reference. All the stars viewed together, the sun included, make out the system's structure. The sun is that structure's physical point of contact. To understand this we must take a look at structure itself.

Every structure reveals at least its outer form. That is what we see when we look at a structured thing. The skeleton for instance is the structure of the human being. That part of our appearance which is due to the skeleton is our outer form.

A structure may also reveal its inner form. That is what we see when we ponder a structured thing, if that thing is composed. The composed human being's inner form becomes available to us when we study all the possible motions and articulations of its skeleton, and observe these in the case of the living human being. The inner form of the human being is revealed best during the dance. It is revealed most naturally while walking, and it is least revealed when the human being is asleep.

The inner form and outer form of a structured being meet at a point of contact. This must be so since form is integral. We cannot possibly imagine how such a point of contact comes about, since it precedes imagination, but we can conceive that it exists. It is responsible for the being's characteristics, and the sum total of all of that being's characteristics make up its character. The point of contact between outer and inner form then is the origin of character. It is the source of stability and of respectability.

21

The name we give to this point of contact in the human body is the organ of copulation. In the male of the species it demonstrates a capacity for both outer and inner form, and in the female it shows a potential for the same. The two in unison are referred to as sex glands.

The exact replica of these is found in the relationship of fixed stars and mobile stars. They mix in relation to each other. The outcome of that mixture is the planets, which compare to the offspring of the two human sexes. Four categories of planets are known and possible. Each of these categories has three definitive characteristics. Each characteristic in turn has two attributes, and every attribute results in a set of properties. This set of properties describes the particular planet.

The purpose of every structure is propagation. But structure is not necessary for propagation. This is why a thing can be reborn, which means that it is destroyed or that its structure falls away, without losing its capacity for propagation. In fact it is not a capacity until after it has been reborn or shaped, being a potentiality previous to that. Realized potential however is not the same as realized capacity. The former ends in a finite thing, while the latter results in infinite things.

Capacity may be realized instantaneously or in time. Potential must be realized contemporaneously. Realized potential is also called talent, and it must be entirely used up before it bears fruit. Realized capacity on the other hand is called glory, and it increases continuously and forever. It may be viewed as grace, as it accrues in time, or it may be seen as holy spirit, as it develops instantaneously. The glory of the structure of the system of heavenly bodies is called the firmament.

Mobile stars differ from fixed stars in that they move with respect to the sun, which is to say in relation to a point of perspective, which is the moon, whereas fixed stars move with respect to the earth, which is to say in reference to a focal point, which is the sun. Fixed stars cannot be seen, but they must be viewed. Mobile stars can be both viewed and seen. Of course this can all be proven in terms of vision and sight, and on the basis of motion, but I leave that to others. The necessary rudiments are found in our philosophy.

All stars are either fixed or mobile, or in a state between the two, such as the sun, which rotates. Rotation is a state of circular motion. It differs from circular motion in general in that the object's path is not fixed but prescribed, and it differs from other states of circular motion, such as revolution for example, in that it continues constantly. Revolution for instance continues inconstantly, which means abruptly or steadily.

The rotation of the sun is periodic. This means that it moves about an irregular point of emphasis. This point of emphasis is the universal centre of gravity. That is where gravity concentrates. Gravity does not have a source or an origin, nor does it have a cause, but it is all three. As a source it produces motion. As an origin it results in weight. As a cause, and more precisely as the cause, since it is the ultimate cause, it succeeds in the effect of reality.

The question what is gravity therefore has three possible answers. One is the effect of gravity; the other is the result of gravity; and yet another is the product of gravity. The question of why is there gravity is simply so that it holds the universe together, which is a manner of speaking, needless to say, and any other of an infinite possibility of manners may do.

The direct result of gravity is energy. As such it mobilizes the body and trains the mind. The trained mind is not the same as the mobilized body, and the two must co-operate in order to remain physical and entire. If they do not cooperate but instead disagree, the body fatigues and the mind tires.

The immediate result of gravity is strength. It has nothing to do with the mind and the body distinct from each other, but it pertains to the physical being. Weakness is simply the absence of strength, and these two are the only case in the universe of two opposites implying each other's absence. They are the replica of the human will. This will either is or it is not, and not unless it is, can it be good or bad, forceful or cowardly, and so on. Strength is a physical property, along with the mind, the soul and the emotions. It either increases or it decreases, but it cannot remain stationary in degree. If it increases it results in power. If it decreases it ends in power. Both in the direction of strength and weakness does power ensue.

The temporary result of gravity is weight. Something has weight only while it is being weighed. Weight applies to the merely physical. It mobilizes the body and organizes the mind, but only insofar as they are expressed. The expressed body is a matter of kinaesthetics, and the expressed mind is a matter of aesthetics. There is such a thing as kinaesthetic sense, which interprets weight in terms of gravity, and appropriates it as knowledge. Such a sense is not proper, but acquired. It is responsible for the phenomenon of levitation. There is also such a thing as an aesthetic sensibility, which is not proper, but appropriated. It is a case of heightened sensibility due to an interaction with weight as a stimulus. Gravity in that case is the stimulant, and the sensitive mind perceives it. Weight is the same wherever an object is weighed. There is no such thing as mass, but that is a label for the purpose of rejecting unidentified appearances of gravity. While mass is unrealized, weight is improper, and it varies from place to place, as it depends on gravity. Once weight has been totally interpreted as it should be, it is in line with gravity and free from it. Consequently it is either measured, or else it can be measured. Since it is useless, if it is not measured, to do anything else with it, and since it is silly, once it has been measured, to measure it again, we may say in the name of good sense that weight is always measured, and that to avoid measuring it is not to create another quantity, such as potential or even inherent weight, nor is it to create another thing, as mass is wrongly supposed to be, but that this is simply an inappropriate thing to do, which deserved to be changed. If it is only altered, it results in inefficiency.

We would like to suggest here that some things which cannot immediately be understood may nevertheless be true, and consequently they can at least be believed. The power of faith is stronger than the faculty of the understanding. If we are wise we do not demand signs of understanding, which must always be disappointing in the end, but instead we rely on the mere quality of truth, which can at least be believed, if not understood.

We wish to apply ourselves now to a study of the relative motion of the planets.

There are seven true planets. They are Mars, Mercury, Venus, Pluto, Neptune, Saturn and Jupiter. Untrue planets are Uranus and the earth. There are also false planets. Presently we want to concern ourselves only with the true planets.

The planets are in obvious configuration. This means that each one is an implicit member of that configuration, which may again be considered to exist as two pairs, as a main member, as a central member, and as a relating or connecting one.

The central number of the planetary configuration is Mars. Its motion is relative and simple. This means that it moves with respect to the earth as a point of reference, and that it revolves in the elementary order of things. It has no axis, but among the planets, and in their configuration, it is the axis. This is in fact why we are able to consider all the planets in relation to one another and as a unified whole. All the other planets depend upon Mars for direction and limitation. Its weight is the greatest of all, and since weight itself is a matter of large and small, we may say that the weight of Mars is colossal. Its size does not interest us here, since it is not part of the configurative relation, but an independent measurement.

The main member of the planetary configuration is Mercury. Its motion is relative and absolute. This means that it revolves with respect to the earth as a point of reference, and with respect to the sun as a focal point, and with respect to the moon as a point of perspective. It is the only planet whose path satisfies all these conditions. Absolute motion cannot be conceived but only imagined. The object in absolute motion seems to be at rest when in fact it moves in a straight line. This is not called a path, but a way. The relative motion of Mercury however is along a path, and this is possible because in the case of this object the path of circular motion and the way of straight motion coincide. Mercury is the only case in the universe of an object moving both in relation and absolutely at one and the same time. As such it is a replica of the human intellect. The intellect is both spontaneous and applied. In application it may be predicted, and spontaneously it may be exploited; and then it may unite with the will in spontaneous application, which avoids prediction and exploitation, but gains correctness and infallibility.

Mercury is the one planet on which all others depend. It is the planetary conductor. It is also a perfect sphere. Why this is necessary for the sake of combined relative and absolute motion can be demonstrated from the shape of the sphere.

The sphere is defined as shape in motion. It is in every direction round. Since shape is devoid of matter, the sphere must be entirely attractive, else it would interfere with the motion on which it depends. The sphere also has no circumference. This is made possible by the object relying entirely on gravity both for inner and outer form, which allows its form to conform to its shape. The sphere is the only object which achieves this, and it is the only thing of its kind in the universe. As such it is the replica of the human brain, which is the plenum.

The sphere is tantamount to perfect fulfilment. Since it is an object, it must be observed in order to be understood. A description of it must be total if it is to succeed. This is the case with the

26

human brain. In order to be understood it must at the same time be exercised, since exercise is its task, and since it depends on this task for its definition. The sphere cannot be conceived out of motion. Neither can it be imagined as a thing. It must first be conceived in motion, and then it may be imagined, but always as a preconceived observation which tends to elude the eye. It must not be grasped if its shape is to be conserved. Once we even attempt to grasp it, a circumference appears and we are not dealing with a sphere, but with a globe.

The globe may be usefully discussed in comparison to the sphere. It is not entirely round. It cannot be defined, because its motion is retrograde. This means that its motion is in reaction to direction. The globe has a circumference, but it cannot be entirely described, because it repulses the imagination. If it did not, the imagination would become involved to its own detriment. There is no such thing as global shape. Also, no two globes are the same. Reaction to directed motion is individual. The globe is the only thing in the universe which exists contrary to existence, and it does this by means of an inversion of essence, which is called entropy. It is because of entropy that the globe can be conceived, but not imagined.

Entropy characterizes the globe, and ectropy characterizes the sphere. The two may be separately studied in their entirety as dimensions of energy. Entropy is a reversal of energy on the basis of inordinate motion. Ectropy is an augmentation of energy on account of retrograde motion. Inordinate motion and retrograde motion, distinctly conceived, cancel each other out. This helps to explain them. In the case of inordinate motion the object relies entirely on its own impulses, and therefore it is said to move mechanically. But there can be no such thing as mechanical motion, but only mechanical movement, since mechanical motion would imply that the machine itself moves, which is absurd. Mechanical movement on the other hand implies that the machine may be moved, which is certainly a possibility.

27

In the case of retrograde motion the object is totally moved. This is difficult to understand because one is accustomed to viewing an object separately from the moving agent and then imagining it in motion. But how can something be an object, we ask, when it is merely viewed? The truth is, that it cannot. It is possible however for movement and objectivity to be simultaneous, and this in the case of the totally moved object, or the sphere.

The totally immovable object is the globe. We might say that it was moved once, and that it conserved the totality of that energy, but of course before it was moved it was not a globe, and after it was moved it was not the same object as was moved. In that direction therefore lies idle speculation. It is the perfect conservation of the globe's energy which gives it its form. Its inner and outer form are always both in contrast and in valance. The contrast lies primarily in the form's dimension, and the balance is due to the unity of dimension. A one-dimensional form is a case of absolute abstraction, and it is the only case of absolute abstraction possible. Form in one dimension is the line. Inner and outer form in the case of the line is always attraction and direction. Inner and outer form in the case of the plane, which is two-dimensional form, by comparison and for example, is extension and inclination or tilt.

While attraction and direction are in contrast, the line is infinite in length, or endless. At the same time the line must be measured, or else it could not have form. And here we come to the very essence of something which is called the magnetic field.

The magnet is the only phenomenon of its kind. Magnetism therefore is not a force, but the force. It is the end-product of the machine, and may be called its output. It does not make sense therefore to inquire into the nature of magnetism by studying its effects, since it is in itself the essence of every effect. Without magnetism there could be no cause. If we wish to discover the essence of magnetism we must study not its effects, but their behaviour.

Effective behaviour is totally self-reliant. It does not depend on a cause, but it is free from it. The one cause of all effective behaviour is perfection. Consequently perfection must precede success. All successive things exist freely and they do not react, but only act. To every successful action there is an opposite and equally successful action. That is the nature of success. Whatever happens in succession differs first of all from all things which happen in sequence in that it is free from its opposite rather than involved with it, to a degree or totally, and secondly it differs from all things which happen as a consequence in that every possible reaction is immediately or instantaneously turned into action or activated, instead of being promoted and to a degree utilized or simply reacted to from the beginning.

Magnetism is successful attraction and repulsion. It compares to gravity, which is successful direction and redirection, in that both gravity and magnetism stem from a common ground, which cannot be given another name however, because it is nothing more or less than magnetism and gravity. Magnetism however is the form of gravity, just as energy is its shape.

The field of magnetism is magnetism viewed in action. It cannot be observed and it has no objectivity. It can be conceived however, and as a result the magnetic field is polarized. This means that attraction and repulsion occur simultaneously.

The polarized magnetic field differs from the unpolarized one in that it is stable. The unpolarized magnetic field fluctuates between dynamic repulsion and static attraction on one hand, and between static repulsion and dynamic attraction on the other. Its force exists, but not mechanically. The great diversion of vacillating force complexes which may occur makes the construction of actual qualities highly improbable. In short, the force of the unpolarized magnetic field is not organized.

The organization of this force is brought about by means of simplification and magnification. The former permits control and the latter determination. Both are necessary prerequisites of what is called the force's centrality. This centrality in turn induces the concentration of lines of force, which create tension and stress. Both tension and stress are aspects of a single thing which is no more than a constitution of such aspects, and which is referred to as a pulse. This pulse is momentary and eternal.

Every pulse is either an impulse or a pulsation, depending on whether it is perceived or received. The impulse is perceived in terms of category or class, and the pulsation is received either as a signal or as a vibration.

What we refer to as the two poles of a polarized magnetic field is merely the appearance of magnetic stability as a result of division into object and thing of an impartial entity. If this division is legitimate, the stability is real and temporary. If the division is premature, the stability is feigned and uncharacteristic. If the division is latent however, the stability is real and permanent. This will be explained in more detail.

An object is observed whereas a thing simply is. An impartial entity differs from an entity in that it is entirely limited. Observation reveals this total limitation. As a thing, its impartiality may be discerned. If we insist either on observing it or upon its impartiality, we distort the recognition process and create a false concept. Out of this false concept then arises a concatenation of fictitious events, which is either useful and applied, or else basically destructive.

If the impartiality is taken for granted and observation is unprepared, becoming mere observance, the intelligence is not satisfied and substitute images are evoked. These are usually accompanied by a fixed idea, which impresses upon them a cloak of unsupportable credibility. The entire process relies on the law, but does not participate in it, and consequently it is legitimate not because it obeys the law, but because it does not disobey it.

Observation and discernment may go hand in hand, just a vision and sight, and this is the recommended approach to the impartial entity. It is called simple cognition, and it corresponds to perception in the case of vision and sight. Cognition accepts the impartial entity on its own grounds and prepares for it a body of knowledge. This means that the total limitation may not be overlooked, but we cannot say that it is observed either, since observation is put entirely at the service of understanding. It also means that the impartiality may not go unnoticed, but we cannot say that it is discerned, since discernment entirely serves the purpose of knowledge. In other words the division into object and thing is latent, and a permanent reality is achieved. This is described as a code of conduct. In actual application it is referred to as the absolute habit. As an experience it is stored as pleasure.

We have said that the impulse of organized force is perceived in terms of category or class. Categorically it appears as electricity, which is defined as current or determined as a charge. In classification it manifests itself as units of work or else as ability to do work. The current of electricity is either direct or alternating, depending on whether it flows through a conductor or across resistance. The electrical charge is either dynamic or static, depending on whether it is contained or retained. Units of work are either counted or accumulated, depending on whether the intention is to proceed or to progress, which will result in a task or in an effort. The ability to do work is either specific or else ordinary, depending on whether energy is expended or also produced, which results in a work or a product.

We also said that the pulsation of organized force is received either as a signal or else as a vibration. The signal is a minimum of communication, and the vibration is a maximum of expression. Expression does not depend upon communication, but communication must rely upon expression. Therefore we receive a signal in a twofold manner, both as a stimulus and as a code. The stimulus is immanently conceptualized and temporarily

31

adopted, while the code is approached interpretatively, but with the end of comprehension in mind, and not for the purpose of independent record. Eventually communication succeeds as a language. This will at another time supply us with the mechanics of language. The vibration is received on its own terms. If it is not, it distorts the optic nerve, and we end up with an inane mixture of waves and particles which paves the cruel road to aesthetic suicide. To accept a vibration on its own terms means to respond to it innocently. This must of course be a pose or an attitude unless our senses have been cleansed. If they have not been cleansed, an integral reception of this novel kind of expression will most quickly bring that end about. The terms on which vibration as an expression proceeds are limited in themselves; therefore there need be no fear of damage or injury. It is such a needless fear which commonly precludes an honest apprehension. This will in time lead to the mechanics of healing and cure.

We have so far touched upon a discussion of Mars and Mercury as the central and main member of the planetary configuration. We remind that we are viewing the planets in relation to each other.

The connecting and relating member of this configuration is Venus. Its planetary path is unique, because it is confined. This means that it proceeds in a predictable fashion, and that Venus moves in conjunction with all other planets. It is not a globe or a sphere, but a combination of both. The properties of a sphere which it holds are those of perfect roundness and of immeasurable dimension. It is a globe however in that it relies upon its own impulses for motion, and in that this motion is a reaction to direction. This double-nature allows Venus both to direct and attract the paths of the other planets, and to influence them in an ambivalent manner. It interconnects all planets in a meaningful way by subjecting them to the inherent limitations of their paths, and it creates in this way a common configurative bond, which allows the configuration of planets to function as a unit. It also creates an interplanetary relationship on the basis of controlled motion, which in this case is motion in terms of a sphere.

We are dealing now with the principal influence which the configuration of planets has as a whole. This influence is metamorphic. The centre towards which this influence is operant is the earth.

Venus is the only thing in the universe which simultaneously unites and divides. As such it is a replica of the human intelligence. In order to know fully the metamorphic influence of the planets in configuration on the earth, and in order to understand this phenomenon distinctly, we must view the intelligence as an aspect of the human being.

As such the intelligence is an isolated case of cognition. It may even be approached as an object. Consequently, since it is mechanically sound, which means that its efficiency is perfect, it may be called a microcosm.

Cosmic refers to a vision of wholeness. It corresponds to the sight of entirety, and the two meet as an understanding of universality. The microcosm therefore simply stands for an instance of universality.

But the intelligence is also a function. This means that it operates and is operated upon. As an aspect, this function is a balancing factor. It mediates between the senses of sight and hearing, and creates an intelligent medium for all the senses, which is called common sense or reason. Within this medium all the senses operate distinctly. But so that no individual sense may create a tyranny of perception over the others, which would result in a fixed idea or in an emotional fixation, the intelligence regulates each distinct sense by reserving the power of instruction, which allows each sense to grow.

This power of instruction which is reserved by the intelligence is called reticence. It may be applied at will. However it cannot be misapplied at will. With respect to this fact the intelligence is not free. On the other hand we cannot say that it is limited or bound, since we perceive through our intelligence the absolute necessity of such regulation of the distinct senses, and are therefore able to employ this lack of freedom to our own advantage. We can use it to exploit the conscience. The result is infinite pleasure.

The conscience, we recall, is not a law, but an apprehension of law, and eventually a comprehension of all law. Once the conscience has achieved priority, meaning that it results directly in the truth, it need not remain passive, but may also become active. As a further result then the truth is successfully revealed. This implies that it is neither metaphorically prefigured, nor logically deduced or induced, but plainly stated.

While the conscience predominates in this manner, the intelligence plays a role. It attracts the attention of the brain and directs the strength of the body. The process is either called teaching or learning, depending on whether the strength of the body culminates, or whether the exercised brain is contracted. A culmination of physical strength is informative, and the contract of the brain is adaptive.

The contract of the brain is a phenomenon which has not until now been discussed. We have spoken of the brain as the plenum. This suggests a totality of dimension. As an organ the brain can be located and observed, for the sake of description and study for example. But the brain is more than an organ. It is the source of all organization, and is itself the master organ. There was a time when this meant that the brain could control mind and body. This was not automatic, of course, and had to be achieved. But once it was achieved, all functions, physical or mental, obeyed one central code of being and behaviour, and needed only to be exposed to that code in order to express themselves accordingly. The connection between the brain and the rest of the body at that time relied to a degree upon the relation of the brain to the mind, but the two were discrete. In other words the body could function while the mind rested, and the mind could operate while the body rested; which is not to claim an especial value for those two joint occupations, but simply to illustrate what is meant by a discreteness of mental and bodily functions due to the accepted control of the brain. As we have said, this was the case at a time. Previous to that time men differed from animals only in that they had a soul, while the mind and body of animals operated conjointly, rather than for the sake of each other. From this earlier or ancient time, which is not historical, to the modern era, which begins with the actual expression of the soul as above discussed, is an inconceivable incident of purely spatial content, which can only be imagined and described. This incident is why time suddenly became historical, rather than remaining a purely natural implication. The human intelligence previous to the modern era was a significant contact with the outside world for the purpose of survival. The phenomenon of incidental space interpreted that contact, and made a contact with the inner workings of mind and body possible, by contracting the brain to the soul. A contract is binding for a purpose. The intelligence could now extend its influence and bring about a balance of mind and body on the basis of a permanent alteration in the human being's structure. If the contract was denied, the human being delayed its advantage. If the contract was only rejected, the human being participated in the contract, but only to a degree. If the contract was approached, but not entirely accepted, the human being had a foretaste of its advantage, but no enjoyment of it. If on the other hand the contract was fully accepted and taken advantage of, the human being reaped a sublime peace, which was called the blessing of the earth.

After a time, which is called the modern age and takes in the first part of the modern era, a second contract of the brain was established. This was not now an incident of spatial content however, but an accident of reality. Consequently time and space both were affected, and historical time was perfected, while space became replete. In terms of the brain itself this constituted a fulfilment. Body and mind were not any more discrete, but actually distinct. The soul consequently received operative powers of its own, due to the sudden productivity of the intelligence as a creative agent. Five aspects of this new contract revealed themselves. The most important one was the reception of the word, which could now demonstrate itself for the first time in its real entirely, instead of merely appearing as a characteristic of language, as during ancient times, or as a structured symbol, as during the modern age. The intelligence operated in terms of this perfect word as the medium of communication, which of course needed to be all-inclusive. The most significant of the five aspects on the other hand was an irrepressible appearance of light, which distinguished sharply between shadow and darkness. Consequently shadow could not any more be confused with darkness, but was connected to its responsible object. But the advantage of this of course was what counted, since now for the first time shadow could be employed to throw the light into relief. This became the task of the arts and the sciences as they were known then. The intelligence with respect to this adamant light functioned as an instrument, which separated and joined: the shadow from darkness in view of the light, and the shadow to the light in its sight. The senses could now begin to rely upon themselves since they were able to appropriate the effusions from the brain due to this second contract, and the mind and the body assimilated. The third and most valuable aspect of the second contraction to the brain was an acceptability of the truth as revealed and as stated. During ancient and still unhistoric times the truth had been able from time to time to put in an appearance. Tribal art attests to this. During the first part of the modern and historic era, which we call the modern age, the truth became available in sign and metaphor. The past was usefully fixed and the future prefigured. As yet the present was not present. It was foreseen in a vision. Due to the second contractual exercise of the brain however, the veil, so to speak, between vision and sight was torn, and the meeting of the two happened. This is an established fact, and not merely a possible occurrence. The realm of the possible begins after this fact. The intelligence, with respect to this consanguinity of sense and experience, could now grow. Maturity became a total concept, not only a conceptual approach. Due to this growing intelligence the distinct mind and body are able to develop freely, while the soul does conscientious work. Stated and revealed truth means a marriage of will and intellect, and the institution of physical being. The mature intelligence grows constantly, and relates all things to each other. The fourth and most readily perceivable aspect of the second brain contract implies a change of experience and leads to a unique way of life. Experience during ancient and primitive times consisted of a coincidence of thought and feeling. We see this especially reflected in the characteristic reaction to such experience as an invention of tools. The tool is principally an established parallel of the effective idea and the affected sense. No interpretation of effect or of affect is required, and certainly no degree of real understanding. The spatial incident upon the organism exposed it to itself. Consciousness was the consequence. An experience of life as a continuity of events became the norm. The intelligence supported this consciousness and interpreted its findings, but could not yet become involved in it in order to achieve an awareness. For this the purposeful death of the human intelligence was required. It is important to stress the actuality of the purpose and to emphasize that in the name of this human death it needed to be the full purpose, and not an approximation or another eventual end. The death of the still static intelligence, or its removal from consciousness, which is the same, was required, so that the substance of the contracted brain could intercede. It manifested itself in terms of the body and in terms of the mind, as these two became distinct, and it was metaphorically referred to as bread and as wine, or, in terms of the intelligence, as my body. This is my body, and it was mentioned at the outset of this science. The intelligence was reborn upon the foundation of this substance, whereupon it could grow. The mutual interdependence of the mind and the body due to their common substantiality made possible their development to maturity and to a physical wholeness. The reborn intelligence, as it is brought back into the divided consciousness which we might describe as consciousness become conscientious or as self-awareness, connects and relates simultaneously the experience of the various senses both to one another and in unity to a developing body of knowledge, which is the human body. This human body is now unanimous with the human soul, as we have suggested in our philosophy, and the unanimity is a fluctuation of contemporary interest. The fifth and most distinct of the five aspects through which we may exercise the brain due to its second contract is a combination of method and technique to which we refer as the way. How life is lived is due in part only to the intelligence, and it is an arbitrating part. To its faculty of connecting and relating corresponds its capacity for decision and choice. The growing intelligence works out of this capacity in collaboration with the will and the intellect. During ancient times however, choice and decision were merely a manner of delineating apparent experience. No reflex was possible, and no ponderable matter needed to be appropriated. Reflection of a purposeful nature became possible with the advent of contemporary history during historic times. The intelligence began to control the elaborations of the brain. Alternative ways not only of behaviour, but also of thought and feeling, became possible and hence a diversity of expression and impression. During the modern age, while the intelligence came to consciousness, the way was either a method or a technique, but it could not be both at the same time, because of the disparity of the will and the intellect. An intelligent method differed from an intelligent technique in that it took account of all available sense data and directed them towards a goal, while the technique acquired the totality of all available information and directed it towards an end. The goal and the end were predictable, and did not necessarily need to be good or even useful. Judgment remained quite a separate function from the method or technique perpetrated. Consequently the intelligence might be satisfied while it was labouring in the name of nonsense just as well as if it were behaving sensibly. Once the brain had been newly contracted however, judgment had become an irrepressible part of all physical functions and actions. What mattered now was solely whether it was good judgment or poor judgment. The former led automatically to an alignment and immediate connection of intellect and will, while the latter inadvertently broke down the unwilling and unthinking being, and prepared it for rebirth. Due to a possible conjunction of judgment and conscience the brain could now be profitably exercised on a continuous basis. The growing intelligence facilitated the demonstration of its result. The way now lay open.

We have viewed the intelligence now as an aspect of the human being and may return to our discussion of the configuration of planets as a whole and of its metamorphic influence on the earth.

The planets are in configuration for the purpose of a particular change which the earth is undergoing. This change is neither cause nor effect of the planetary configuration, but it concurs with it. Neither the change nor the configuration can be understood separately.

The earth is in the process of becoming a sphere. The conditions under which a sphere can actually exist must be purely elementary. This implies a relationship of all visible things under the eightfold pattern of description, as set forth in our philosophy. The singular essence of such a state of being is human subsistence. Subsistence differs from existence in that essence is not understood but implicit. Human subsistence implies the sovereignty of human being.

The metamorphosis of the earth is first of all a transformation, and then a transubstantiation. Both of these terms are fully explained in our philosophy. The earth began as a structured thing. It was built up from particles of resistance according to the standard of existence itself. Needless to say this standard cannot be described, but only alluded to. As a structural thing, which is to say as structure, since we are dealing with the earth and the centre of the universe, the earth reacted to movement. This is the same as to say that its particles resisted. The totality of this resistance formed a contingency of matter.

All matter results in motion, unless this motion is immediately transformed. The motion of the earth as material structure never reached the terminal stage which would allow us to refer to it. It was immediately transformed into a concatenation of elementary states. Of these states there are eight. They are combustion and fermentation; evaporation and condensation: desiccation and solidification; and decomposition and putrefaction. Analogous to these were the four early elements of fire, water, air and earth. Each of the eight states was united with its opposite and then became a process.

All this corresponded to an alignment of the planets in separate orbits as particles of resistance to motion. Matter formed itself in response to motion, and consequently all orbits were interlinked.

The stars accumulated as particles of resistance to light. Their matter consequently is not formed at all, but either sedimentary or in flux, or a combination of both.

During the collection of resistant particles as earth, planets and stars, gravity could be defined as the total resistance of all these particles, whether to movement, to motion or to the light. Gravity was the common denominator of all centres of resistance, and light was the common environment. Since the particular resistance of the stars was of another nature, they remained uninvolved in the transformation of the earth, and only reflected all available energy. Consequently the terrestrial change which we are describing could remain energetically self-sufficient.

The energy therefore which was available to the interaction of the planets with the earth was both inherent and reflected. The configuration of the planets coincided with the transformation of the earth as a series of unified processes. Subsequently it is not possible to speak of planetary orbits or of elementary states. The former would be dated and the latter uninformed. Only a record of these events still exists in the indistinct imagination.

A study of the unified elementary processes of transformation will yield the same results as an inquiry into the modes and indices of planetary configuration, since each one wholly involves and implies the other. For the sake of clarity we will undertake both.

Combustion and fermentation are unified processes. One cannot go on without the other one going on. Combustion is defined as the atmospheric break-down of matter into temperature and heat. This gives us an idea of how these two processes are linked. The break-down of matter as such is not a process but a procedure. It must happen in time. Every procedure therefore has an aim and there is a logical reason for it. The logical reason for the breakdown of matter is the distribution and rearrangement of matter. The former is a good reason and the latter the right reason. We distinguish between the two so as to avoid all unapplied logic.

The process of combustion is limited by the procedure of material breakdown, and the process of fermentation arises from that procedure. Of the two unified processes combustion is the endemic one, and fermentation is the exegetic one. Endemic refers more specifically to the permutation of combustible material, and exegetic refers more specifically to the perpetration of fermenting material. It is important to notice here that fermentation is a dynamic process, whereas combustion is not. Combustion is a process of inversion. It is explained in the following manner. Atmosphere is the mixture of ether and air. Ether and air are its two ingredients. They are both agents of dispersion. Dispersion is the interaction of something more dense with something less dense. Nothing is less dense than ether. It is therefore called the agent of dispersion. Air is not immaterial, but it is less dense than any matter which can be broken down. Atmosphere, by the way, is always in mixture, and its two ingredients never coalesce. Both of these intersperse with the combustible martial and render it less dense. This means primarily a situation of the resistant particles, due to the tendency of the interspersing atmospheric ingredients of ether and air to remain in mixture, and secondarily it means a dissolution of particular resistance itself, due to the centrifugal force of the interspersed atmospheric mixture, which conditions the particles by eliciting from them an attractive property. Once situated and conditioned in this manner the particles of resistance have become instants of gravity, which have nothing in common with their previous resistant particularity except their number, which is the same.

It should be noted as an important aside here that particles of resistance are resistant particles, but not resisting particles, and that particular resistance is resistant particularity, but not resisting particularity. There is such a thing as resisting particles and as resisting particularity, but it is a ridiculous thing and not worthy of more than mention here, since it is not observed or an entity of observation, but a result of observance, which is an abuse of reality.

A number of instants of gravity is the logical outcome of every procedure of material break-down. It remains for a time. This time is called a logical interval, and cannot be any further broken down. In experience it must be waited out. Under observation it yields a modicum of patience. As a thing in itself it cannot be viewed, but only seen. Each separate instant of gravity lasts for the logical time interval, and becomes an instance of gravity. The total number of gravitational instants during the logical time interval turns into a gravitational field. A gravitational field is the compendium of a set number of gravitational instances. The gravitational field per se is the compendium of all available gravitational instances, and when it is viewed it is in configuration. Instances of gravitation are then approached as indices of configuration, or else they are observed as modes of configuration. If these modes and indices are studied in terms of the heavenly bodies, we are dealing with the case of planetary configuration. The modes of configuration are the planets themselves, and the indices of configuration are their implicit and explicit properties of motion.

Every planet moves according to its inherent force impulses. This is the same as to say that every planet is moved by design of primitive magnetic attraction. Implicit properties of motion differ from explicit properties of motion in that they are otherwise expressed. Since both expressions exist it will not do to disregard one of them.

To move and to be moved is one and the same thing. Motion implies that either may be the case. A mode is a duality of expression. A mode of configuration therefore reveals the truth about the purpose of configuration by supplying us on one hand with an imprint of configurative behaviour, and on the other hand by allowing us to gain possession of the catalyst by means of which we are able to ponder the very essence of configuration, planetary or otherwise, and to plumb its meaning. This catalyst is the essence of modality, which is radiation.

We will discuss the planet Neptune as a mode of planetary configuration. Its power of radiation is greatest among the seven planets. For that reason it may be used as a key in the study of configuration itself.

When we gaze at this planet we become conscious of a peculiar phenomenon which is described as a vortex. A spiral motion seems to attract us towards its centre, which becomes blurred to the vision.

When we look at this phenomenon, its attraction increases rapidly. The spiral motion seems to draw us in, and we may sense an unpleasant demand upon our organ of sight.

A bit of understanding is not required. If we wish to pursue an experiment, we might affirm the force of attraction which we perceive, and we might make ourselves totally accessible to it. If on the other hand we wish merely to observe the phenomenon, we must allow our senses to become totally receptive, which excludes eventually all anxiety and reticence of appreciation. Under the circumstances of the present study we will first experiment, and then turn our attention to the object itself.

The cause of the spiral motion seems to lie at the centre. Therefore we apply ourselves to that position. It happens that our vision clears as soon as we corroborate it by sight. Now we feel that our attention is drawn in three different directions at once. The attempt to create a concept yields three sorts of spiral motion. The first is vertical spiral motion. The third sort of spiral motion is vorticose. These are interpreted, and as a result we feel pleasure. We are not aware of any spiral motion as such, but we know that our situation has not changed, and consequently we induce, by means of verbal exercise, the state of the brain. This means that we have identified fully with our phenomenon of the vortex, and that we may expect the experiment's success. The state of the brain is constant introversion. This implies a mastered cohesion of body and mind, and a simultaneous proficiency of the working soul. The brain as the plenum reflects correctly and exactly in this state the phenomenon as a replica. The vortex emerges as a type of motion, and as the only type of motion that can be at once seen and envisioned. This makes it the only thing in the universe that simultaneously moves and creates motion, and as such it is the exact replica of the human instinct.

Before we turn to the task of observing what we have presently identified with experimentally, we will make a study of the human instinct, both as a faculty and as a function.

Instinct is the essence of life. As such it prefigures life. We recall from our philosophy that a figure is an instrument of terminal arrest. Both internally and externally the human being masters this figure in the strictest confidence. It is the secret of life, and it is sacred.

All living things which are also alive, meaning that they do not only appear to be living, are instinctively inclined and have instinctive tendencies. Only the human being is able to master these tendencies and inclinations, and only the man actually does. Human instinct is unique in that the human being (man) has it. This gives him the capacity to manipulate himself. If he develops this capacity he gains mastery over all lesser forms of life. The human being is able to gain mastery of, but not over himself and other human beings.

By forms of life is meant the various, diverse, and manifold manifestation of the essence of life. This is instinct inhabited. Only habitual instinct extends terminally and unfolds lawfully, both at the same time. Those are the two prerequisites of the single organism.

An organism is an assortment of organic functions and capacities in a self-sufficient working order. Organic refers to self-imposed limitations of an environment. Self-sufficiency implies total dependence.

Every self-sufficient being is instinctively intact. This is the same as to say that it is mechanically sound. The habitual instinct is the motor of the mechanically sound being. A motor is defined in terms of motion as motion incarnate

There is no such thing as natural law, or as natural laws. What is sometimes labelled as such is an inherently unsuccessful attempt to impose and impress the results of incoherent abstraction upon something which in fact does not follow a law and indeed can never abide by law. Nature is either imagination and fantasy, or else essence and existence, depending on whether we observe it or experience it. Law is an aspect of reality, and reality differs from nature a man does from woman. To impose laws upon nature is the same as to coerce one's wife to obedience. The logical outcome is that one ends up either with no woman or else with no wife; and the same goes for nature. Nature is susceptible only to love, and love overrules all law, even if it does not always fulfil it.

The abiding principle of nature is the figure. This means that the course of nature is figurative. When reality poses a problem, it can be solved, but in the case of nature the problem must be figured out. Every single organism, whether animal, vegetable or mineral, may be viewed very usefully as a problem posed by reality which nature has figured out. But an answer is not yet a solution.

Instinct is entirely dependent upon time. Our experience of time characterizes our instinctive behaviour. In ancient and prehistoric times, before the beginning of the modern era, man inhabited his instinct prematurely. This allowed him to resist with singular vehemence not only reality, but also the influence of nature. That he chose to resist rather than to comply was the cause of that prematurity. An elaborate attitude of disbelief towards all appearances was its belated effect.

Time was experience then only as a hindrance. An immediate vision of reality was felt rather than comprehended, and that feeling was mistaken for a means towards an end. Nature was understood only as an environment, and consequently all concepts which were formed were empty, which led to an aberrational exploitation of nature. History did not exist. Reflection therefore was either wilful or intellectual, but never both at once or in unison. Instinctive tendencies, operated on by the intellect, fell away and were discarded as injurious to a tranquil state of mind. This resulted in unjustified anger and wrath. Instinctive inclinations pondered by the intellect aggravated the false contentment of the body and were disregarded as harmful. This ended in acute impatience and vainly jealous zeal. Instinctive inclinations suffered by the will were projected stubbornly into surrounding objects which were treated previously as subjects and subsequently as idols. A fragmentation of human integrity ensued, with its usual symptoms of ill-directed hatred and violence. Instinctive tendencies borne up by the will were loosely fitted together in terms of the reality and nature which were being resisted, and this reactionary construct of anxious cerebration and chronic emotionality constituted the commencement of the world.

The beginning of the modern age was marked by a self-consciousness of instinctive behaviour. Man began to compare himself to other organisms on the basis of such instinctive behaviour. The world became a special inducement for the betterment of character. The first glimpses of personality broke through. Instinctive tendencies and inclinations were now seen in the light of race and tribe. Race is defined as an original expression of popular consent to the cultivation of instinctive urges. An urge is instinctively inclined and tends to make proper use of the world. A tribe is defined as a umber of people who cultivate inherited notions of law and order in terms of the world, and pass them on by generation. A notion is a partial concept of an instinctive moment. With the event of told time, or history, instinct could become reflective, which opened the door to planned malice and to cosmic thought. The latter led to a view of the world in terms of popular illusion, and hence to the first great religions and works of art. The former tempted this and brought it to proof.

As soon as history came to its natural conclusion with the event of eternal time at the end of the modern age a connection was established between instinctive tendency and inclination, so that henceforth one would by necessity imply the other. The instinctive urge was now related to the world in all experience, and its rejection meant a tie with the world, while its acceptance meant a tie with nature. In terms of social function this made possible the duality of author and priest, and of criminal and sinner. Intuitive grasp combined with instinctive apprehension to produce the mystic and the heretic on one hand, and the genius and the outlaw on the other. The man of the world became civilized, due to his recognition of the duality of instinct and reason, while the man of nature became cultured due to his understanding of the possible link of instinct with reason. Education raised the one out of misery, and learning lowered the other away from vain pride.

Modern times culminate in the compression of instinct and reason into units of life or physical cells. The instinctive urge is not only accepted, but worked out. Revelation is possible, an act of reasonably instinctive demonstration in the face of the world. All things are possible in terms of each other. A common basis is achieved for instinct, intelligence, intuition and intellect due to the spontaneous regeneration of free will in terms of the incarnate soul. History is possible as a simple repetition of the truth, which allows for a type of reflection both creative and scientific. Finally instinct is a habit now also in the case of man, which returns him to his intended state of universal mastery, at one with the birds of the air and the lilies of the field.

We are in the position now to observe the phenomenon which we identified with experimentally, previous to our discussion of human instinct. We recall that we described it as vortex.

As an object the vortex is a profusion of elementary states. These states are captivated. This means that they are united under a single concept and based upon a unique substance. The substance is called gravitational pull, and the concept is number.

The concept of number always implies categorically the two concepts of numeral and integer. By the same token does the substance of gravitational pull always infer the substance of attraction and direction. Implication is a function of the concept, while inference is the instrumentality of substance.

The implication of the numeral is the differential calculus. It is able to work out the objective reality of a set of partially known circumstances. These circumstances must be either real or natural to begin with. If they are artificial or perverse, the differential calculus must fail. It does fail in terms of mere appearances or on account of mere logic. Whenever it fails, it ends either in imponderability or else in the void. In either case it must then be categorically overcome.

The attractive substance of gravitational pull is figured out by means of metaphor. The metaphor is its simple limitation. It operates strictly upon the figure of the phenomenon, and either interprets it or else extends it. Its interpretation is the symbol, and its extension is the sign. Both the symbol and the sign are metaphorical. They must be made use of immediately, and not applied. The proficient metaphor is either appropriated or else assimilated. If it is applied, the metaphor is false. In that case it must be rejected. If it is not rejected, it contributes to the breakdown of structured matter. Both the symbol and the sign may be applied or assimilated. The assimilated symbol is a device, either for the transmission of information of for the transport of illusion. The appropriated sign is a sense of stimulus, either as an aid to vision or as an improvement on sight. The appropriated symbol is a physical inducement, which either works on the body as a factor of knowledge, or on the mind in terms of insight. The assimilated sign is either a mode of expression or a manner of communication, such as painting and the composition of music, or gesture and language.

The directive substance of gravitational pull is either graphic or schematic. In the case of the graph there is an application of order either through control or by means of design. In the case of the scheme either theory or hypothesis forms a basis of regulation, or else manipulation according to a plan brings about an orderly alteration or change. Gravitational pull is either direct, or else it directs. Directly it operates in a manner or in a fashion.

This means that no motive is required and no end is posited. Often this is referred to as blind motion or commotion. It is not without a purpose however, though its purpose is always implicit. If it directs, gravitational pull is either a motivation or else a field. This means that it operates spontaneously or in terms of environment.

The concept of the integer implies the integral calculus. It is an expression of the incarnate mind. When we count, we eliminate progressively the possibility of a number of things from their reality, in order to gain certainty of possession. Counting is either logarithmic, when it is physical, or else it is arithmetic, when it is mental, and applied methodically or as a technique. Physical counting is creative. It is the essence of style. It is essentially the repetition of whole entities for the sake of pure progress. Counting serially in integers then is a case of total and complete variation. No one number has anything in common with another. The integral calculus pursued in this direction yields up the total analysis of physically contrived data and reconstructs them on the basis of reality. All geometry is an application of the physical integral calculus. Measurement is abstracted and demonstrated in the concrete by means of illusion. The result is meant as a vehicle of contemplation. If it is again applied it becomes an exercise in the preposterous, which compares to the harnessing of a thoroughbred horse to the wrong end of a wagon so that it might produce milk.

The elementary states of which the vortex is composed are diverse in interest and manifold in conception. They combine with each other to produce events of an elementary nature. Such events for instance make up the conditions of the atmosphere and more particularly they are responsible for what we call weather. By this we do not mean to suggest that the atmosphere and the weather of the earth are influenced or regulated by the planet Neptune. It would be as silly to suggest the opposite. We do wish to point out however that the vortex is a universal concept, and a phenomenon which may be recognized in the case of the planet Neptune, and observed in detail in the workings of the atmosphere of the earth.

Elementary events are not profitably classified. Their classification is a matter of convention. What corresponds to them are the surface conditions of the earth. Consequently they may be studied in themselves, in interaction and conflux, and they may be described in terms of topography, politics, language and so on. it is also possible to capitalize on the correspondence between the two, which yields a science of the brain. This may be explained as follows. Since the brain is the plenum, it is the only case in the universe of the ideal corresponding precisely to reality. In other words the ideal brain is also the real brain. But since the brain is inside of our head, we cannot do better than to study it in reflection. Now the kind of correspondence which is unique to the brain is that of the means with the end. The end of man's life however is the pleasure of living on earth, and the means towards the achievement of that end lie within the power of his own understanding. The profusion of elementary events and the surface conditions of the earth are the only case in the universe of exact correspondence. This makes them the replica of the human brain. To study this case of exact correspondence, and to study it in reflection, which is no special effort, since that is the only way it can be studied at any rate – this means to understand the brain, which is the only case of precise correspondence. That the understanding of his brain furnishes man coincidentally with that most valuable knowledge of his own environment might be more surprising if we doubted that the surface of the earth were man's original and most advantageous habitat.

That aspect of the human being which lends itself to a study in terms of mechanical law is the emotions. All the emotions of which the human being is capable are called his emotional life. This is in itself a force and a potential instrument of love. If we study the emotional life as a force, we recognize how it is based upon love, and we see it in opposition to the rational mind. If we study the emotional life as an instrument, we realize that it involves the rational mind, and we understand it as a function of brain power.

The one emotion towards which all others aspire is joy. Joy is also the basic ingredient of happiness. The single law of mechanics from which all others arise is the law of special relativity. It states that all related things behave so as to remain in energetic harmony. By energetic harmony is meant an equal presence of energy in all parts. When we contemplate now the essence of all being and notice how humanity is involved in all things, we may profitably compare the emotional life to all the forces of nature, and then we comprehend how the two are in fact one and the same, on one hand viewed as exterior to the person, and on the other hand seen from within. Just as nature is necessarily developed towards reality, so is the emotional life liked to the attributes of personality.

All the forces of nature conform to the laws of mechanics. The central force of nature, upon which all the others depend, is the force of growth, which is called generation. In order to be generated, the nature of a thing must be reversible. By reversible nature is meant the capacity to sustain mechanical change. Such change is mechanical which does not depend upon outside forces, and whose process has a definite end. The process with a definite end is called progress. When the end is not adhered to or striven towards we speak of regress. That law of mechanics due to which all forces of nature remain in constant equilibrium is called the general law of energetic momentum. By energetic momentum is meant the innate drive to remain in motion.

We will set forth now the first shape, which translates natural force into emotional force. It is called a shape because it communicates immediately a reality which is equally personal and natural. This is the shape: Force is the capacity for illusion. Shapes are made use of as things in themselves. This means that they have no applicability whatsoever, and that their value lies in the success of communication itself. For a shape to be, each of its components must be definable in terms of the other, and neither definition may to any degree involve the other. Hence we define force in terms of illusion as the significant material impulse for an increase in dimension, and we define illusion in terms of force as sufficient content for the purpose of making an individual being whole.

The concept of the vacuum is of importance here. We know that every vacuum is a comparative entity, and yet we are able to view the cosmos, and that which it is not. Consequently the anticipated vacuum in itself, which we know cannot be, must reside intrinsically in the act of vision. It is the illusion which has been exploited, but not discharged of its ideal content. Every vision, and every act of vision, simulates the idea. In the same way one might mistake something for the thing in itself, which cannot be, when the seen thing has been categorically depleted, but not yet rendered devoid of form. Every seen thing approximates the form, and when we speak of the form and of the idea we are dealing with the absolute reality potential, on one hand as the mind perceives it, and on the other hand as the body feels it, and the two must be drawn fully into consideration if we decide to create perfect work. Ideal residue sets up an inhibition of falsehood and a formal remnant manages to forestall precision. Hence we categorize not on the basis of reason, but in the light of reason, so that the latter is the medium per se, and we do not calculate so as to be correct, but for the sake of the instilled purpose, which is singular and earthly. The medium exists, being the totality of all things in themselves, and the purpose exists, being the three-dimensional cosmos in the light of day, but the thing in itself and the vacuum in itself do not exist, nor are they meant to. Wherever something comes into existence, which is not the same as to say that it comes about, or into being, it resists nothing on one hand, and on the other hand it involves being totally. The essence of whatever exists is not necessarily apparent. It is possible for something merely to exist, which means that it survives and does not contribute in any way to anything. Such mere existence has come to a stop. Its bare continuation in time was a function of the developing cosmos, and a tool, so to speak, by means of which all things had to be limited while there was yet a chance of fragmentary existence. With the endowment of human existence with necessary goodness, or, to put it in other words, with the event of perfect communication in reality and in the light of day, meaning having become flesh and blood, existence is henceforth either essential or not at all.

It remains to clarify what is meant by mechanical change. Only such things can undergo mechanical change whose attributes are free. An attribute is free when it describes the thing to which it has been attached. Of course an attribute cannot both describe a thing and be attached to it, at the same time. But since time is whole and not at all any more either discontinuous or interrupted, we may speak of an instance of time consumption, which for the sake of precision is called an instant, when the attached attribute becomes descriptive, during the process of communication or as the result of explicit statement.

If mechanical change is viewed in terms of human experience, and especially of the human experience of energy, it may be perceived outside of us, immaterial in concept and casual in manner, and at the same time influentially constructed.

This construction is substantially integral. We may picture it as a confluence of visible parts that appeal to our interest. Intentionally we may do nothing here. The intention we would express however is gathered within, in the interest of positive continuity.

The step from construction to structure is a controversial one. Existentially there can be no doubt as to the material acceptability of that which is not yet experience but experience in substance. What this is, how it is, can only be assumed, but that it is cannot be doubted. Experience in substance, we say, is mechanically involved.

The study of mechanical involution is an intriguing one. The subject should not be confused with the increment of mental apparatus, a delusion so dear to the extinct sciences. Mechanical involution may be said to bring down to earth all sensible representations of present life, for the sake of whatever fulfilment of promised reality that may still be our wish. Inventive speculation and the provoked possibility are not to be excluded. There is an increment of wisdom however that cannot be denied. It behaves automatically. Upon the issue of this wisdom the human being is made once and for all susceptible to the truth and invulnerable to falsehood.

There is naturally also a built-in fear before what we have called this experience in substance. Mechanical involution bypasses this fear, on account, again naturally, of each increment of wisdom, while the wisdom, viewed quantitatively, is due to the mechanical process vividly imbibed.

One may wish to secure, for example, a straight line consequence of sensible parameters, in whatever sphere of experience one cares to mention, and this kind of infinite magnitude of success, so frequently a stumbling-block to our terrestrial endeavours, a scandal to our ambitions in society, all too easily imagined and all too soon mismanaged, suddenly shows itself to have been for some time in gradual operation where we could not include it because we were otherwise inclined. We discover, in short, that our luck is phenomenal and that we have indubitably made it.

We come now to a final recognition of what can only be called the machine in man. It operates within us to the exclusion of a self or of an ego, and this is at once its main task and the primary source of its definition.

The machine in man is automatic. Its various properties explain our behaviour when under duress. We are in fact under duress when our intentions surpass our limitations; when we intend beyond our capacity, such as during the process of learning, or when we create.

Our machine: our mechanical aptitudes – bring us into contact with a greater degree of reality and make accessible for us a more profound sense of nature. What follows then is a matter for wisdom and intelligence. A more profound sense of nature requires wisdom for it to culminate in habitual conduct rather than to dissipate itself as mere cravings and drives. Contact with a greater degree of reality calls for intelligence so that work, deeds and action, are the outcome, not mere fantasy and dream.

The machine in man may also be viewed as a case of mature feeling. Understanding is needed for this. The terminology for discourse on this topic is itself contrived.

Most of us would agree that it is possible to surround a particular subject with feeling, or by feeling, in a way that limits that subject towards a particular end. The end must remain undefined as such but the feeling may assume modes of expression, of presentation. Consequently one may be granted the type of insight into that subject which acts automatically, though with due reference to likely appearances, which cannot be explained, only demonstrated. There are, then, manifestations of the machine in man insofar as we supply one another with the right to oriented subjective feeling. The orientation of the feeling, of course, is not possible in separation from the right, but it may be observed distinctly, one from the other, while an insight takes place.

One supposes quite naturally that a sort of reflective reverence is due to this mechanical performance as a whole, and indeed such a response is most frequently elicited. We penetrate the obscurity of a judged subject and find we are in the presence of judgment. For a while illusions will keep us entertained.

Take the wheel for example. Here we have a case of motor illusion that combines the concept of oneness with that of distance. We call it a motor illusion because it illustrates uniquely the basic idea of a drive. Here we come face to face with the original use of all of our mechanical contrivances, before we began to apply them to one another as though they were things in themselves. Every mechanical contrivance as such reflects a human reality, and this should be the area of its use and application.

The wheel, for example, allows us to play with the idea of special drive against resistance to gravity. While gravity is resisted, as in the case of weight, there is an equal and opposite insistence on material production. We might say that regardless of which comes first, each begets the other.

Not until we isolate the machine from the human being, an extravagance at best and a downright mischief at its worst, does the resistance to gravity become independent, supererogatory, and eventually transitive to the point of fatuity. The insistence on material production at the same time tends to spend itself, to inflate artificially our capacity for material intake, to proliferate means as though they were ends, and finally to legislate in favour of a perverse belief in mere magnitude and multitude.

Therefore we should not apply the wheel, in our thinking, to the lever, for example. While the wheel combines the concepts of oneness and distance, the lever has practical application as its motive, so that oneness and distance are not combined as concepts but visually performed in fact. We are really dealing with different levels of experience, and the difference exists for the purpose of renewal in mind and body. When we pretend and act as though the difference did not exist we shut ourselves off from the machine and force it into an external betrayal of itself.

Let us look at this difference in levels of experience more closely. The wheel illustrates satisfactorily the useful and sufficient independence of static forces from dynamic fields or planes. Static forces have no corrigible illusion to maintain and consequently we rely on them as means of abstraction, as less-than- conscious areas of organic activity which may help to explain or hinder temporary infidelities to the mechanical law.

By the mechanical law we simply mean the mutual exchange of action and matter. Action relates to matter in the same way as matter relates to action; begin with one and end with the other. A thorough comprehension of the mechanical law institutes perfect biological attributes.

Dynamic fields are always to be adjusted, on account of purposes, or maintained, in line with a particular determination. However this comes about, through a diffusion of elementary particles or extremely perpetrated, one has an eye to the constitution of the thing while final points of view are entertained, engaged, involved, etc., as primary, secondary and so on.

Without undertaking an autopsy of extinct mechanics, we may eliminate the usual side-by-side exigencies of terminal experience-clusters that have come to overrun the scientific endeavours of the mind. One cannot any more behave as though impracticalities were to guide us through crowds of imponderables into a society of impossibilities, all for the sake of energy expended and mere brain used.

The machine as a contrivance is probably as difficult to imagine as its intellectual counterpart, the machine as an organ. An understanding of the mechanical law allows us to distinguish intelligently between the two while at the same time avoiding the divorce of either from their common root of motion, their similar status in terms of human response to gravity.

The machine as an organ, as a sufficient contract of forces whose common aim centres on exploitation of material values and on exploration of material entities, when it is studied with a view to its ultimate perfection, has definite characteristics by which it may be recognized, and we chose to do so only because we believe that the perfect machine, if not the perfected machine, is able by its very existence to transcend mater, thereby rendering it bountiful.

While the gradual, stage by stage, level upon level of perfection of the machine as an organ must not necessarily be computed or consciously followed up, it is of great importance that we habitually familiarize ourselves with this ultimate purpose of the machine as the transcendence of matter.

We can see simply by looking around us and by questioning our feeling on this: that bountiful matter does not somehow fit into the same category with all that the word matter implies. And yet we feel constrained, by our essential make-up as creatures, to evaluate matter as such, to estimate its worth in the light of our eternal existence, and finally to judge in accordance with the perfect life we have inherited and upon which we continue to draw.

The grasp, intuitive or in whatever fashion, on and of our perfect, eternal and original inherited life; the perfection of the machine in view of this; the transcendence of matter for the sake of bountiful matter: these related points shall continue to occupy our concentration for the remainder of this science. A discussion of the mechanical law as such should not be necessary since we intend to keep it utterly in operation as a complete thing, fulfilled and fulfilling in its own way.

Matter may be said to be bountiful when it translates readily into knowledge and understanding. There is no end to bountiful matter itself, but its end lies in knowledge and understanding as such. While it occurs to us, therefore, to experience matter in its own light, to locate material points here or there, then or now, we exercise the limits of extinction.

Extinct matter, metaphorically speaking, attempts to rest in itself and always, everywhere, fails to do so. We cannot speak of extinct matter except metaphorically. However extinct matter may become instinct, and this is extremely important, important as an extreme.

Our instinctive behaviour vis-à-vis extinct matter may – not must – but may entail an act of violence which in turn may be described from without. Since instinctive behaviour carries along with it a reasonable form of conduct, we may describe this act of violence as instinctive behaviour going against reasonable forms of conduct, however such a description is proximate at best.

We must remember that extinct matter is shapeless and that it embodies the tension between chaos and order and manifests the stress of structure on stuff. It has no existence of sorts except under duress and its essence must remain difficult. We do well to keep in mind, therefore, what we may expect and what not. The search for truth in extinct matter is always a case of mistaken identity. The instruments themselves which we use to avail ourselves of knowledge and understanding, of sense and corporeality, are either extinct or live, and once we have rejected extinct instruments and have made it a habit to insist on measurement within the framework of distinct species rather than as a repetitive end in itself in the hope of controlling and harnessing chimaera, we soon develop a taste for discrimination. This taste for discrimination does the actual work, in terms of human being.

Extinct matter, we should realize, excludes the very essence of being, which is humanity. Since those who involve themselves with extinct matter become extinct themselves, we may talk about it in this fashion: that it never quite succeeds in ridding itself of humanity altogether but that it defines its parameters of eventual exactitude by the continuous effort to do so. Extinct matter, in other words, can never become quite impersonal, while bountiful matter is in fact a person.

Once we have come to know this person we like to remain in her vicinity. She takes care of us as though we were her own children, and in truth we are her children. But how can matter be a person, and why female? Equally, why should truth be a person, and male? Every individual person might ask him- or herself how it comes that he or she is a person rather than a thing or an entity or a body, and why she is female and he male.

This has to do with the developing nature of reality, nothing less, nothing more. There is such a thing a universal growth, whereby whatever is also becomes. We know that the essence of being is humanity and this lets us contemplate the nature of human being and its fruit, the human being. You and I are human beings, two in number, and our special meaning to each other and for each other is our personality. If I love you, I do it in terms of my personality. If we love one another, our two personalities become one.

If we agree that the essence of being is humanity, then we shall also agree that what we become is essentially divine. We would say that the essence of becoming is divinity if it were not for the fact that becoming, unlike being, cannot be understood as such but always entails to a degree or to some measure that which becomes. So while it would by no means be wrong to state that the essence of becoming is divinity, it would be misleading under some circumstances and so we insist that the essence of becoming is divine.

Whatever anything becomes, however, has as its principle feature an exact momentum of growth, which itself becomes what it is, and so we may approach the special individual in the light of terrestrial and mechanical aspects of change. To put it another way, in order to attain a real knowledge of someone or some one thing we take carefully into account not only what is but also what he, or she, or it becomes. Since what we have called the momentum of growth is exact, it makes no difference whether we study it, phenomenally or environmentally, or take it upon ourselves as an entirely subjective point of view. We make no effort to comprehend such a thing in isolation, but recognize it as much in ourselves as in others, as much within as without, and it is in fact a most fitting application of life within and without: this mechanical concept of an exact momentum of growth, along with its counterpart, the particular physical moment.

The special individual, therefore, viewed mechanically, be it person, thing, body, entity or whatever, is available to us as a particular physical moment and as an exact momentum of growth.

Whatever we make, we move, and what is made is in motion. We take pride and joy in our ability to view, not the world, nor the universe, nor things, but everything, mechanically. Everything is not the world or the universe, as extinct science, off and on, would have it, but everything is unlimited, and we have cause to be happy that indeed everything is at our disposal. We cannot define everything because of its incarnate state. But everything is made and therefore in motion. This gives us a good and useful idea of everything.

This idea of everything is called the ideal, and when something is viewed mechanically we build up our idea of everything, a little at a time.

We can say, therefore, that everything is all special individuals, and that every special individual has a concrete identity. Please remember that we do not mean individuals, but special individuals, and not individual things but special individuals.

The concrete identity of a special individual is more or less in evidence but it is always and everywhere established so that we need not interfere in order to make contact, for example, nor do we intrude with impunity where an established identity holds sway. We are, after all, dealing with that which is made, and consequently there is inherent purpose, vicarious meaning, direction and attraction of attributes, and so on. Something made is not something fabricated or something botched.

This becomes emphatic in what we called the particular physical moment. Here it depends on us how far an experience leads to greater enlightenment. Not mind alone, nor body alone, but both in one, compare to the particular moment, and if we care to adopt the role of an observed, a favourite pastime of the extinct scientist, we still posit ourselves then as special individuals with a concrete identity, becoming part and parcel of circumstances in which we have elected to view something mechanically. If a clock is supposed to play a part, then we predicate that clock within as without. If we wish to view something inert mechanically, fine and dandy, nothing wrong with that, as long as we remain aware throughout of our own comparative inertness. For this is the whole point of live mechanics, not to operate humanity out of being, but to view the essence of being as made, or in the making.

The special individual as a particular physical moment may be pondered. A cup, a thing, a body, you, time: these may all be pondered, if they are special individuals, each as a particular physical moment. Anything may be pondered under those circumstances. This ponderability may be looked for as a test, for what we find imponderable may not be a special individual, or we may not be viewing it mechanically. If we view God mechanically he becomes available to us as the particular physical moment of Jesus Christ, whom we may ponder, whence derives our enjoyment of his presence as truth, life, light, word and way. Or we may view the word mechanically and it will become available to us as the particular physical moment of incarnate speech personified.

More important, of course, than testing whether or not something is in fact something, than testing via ponderance for the special individuality of something, is what we can actually come up with when we ponder it. There is enough for a live science to understand without turning back in on itself. The field, as a matter of fact, is infinitely large, which means that it cannot be summed up and filed away and gloated over, and also that we can relax, since no one can get there first and beat us to a prize. There is more than enough for everyone and then much left over.

The special individual pondered as a particular physical moment reveals its concrete identity and joins us in the world. This is of course the end of mechanical science and our overall reason for its pursuit. Deep down we want everything to join us in the world, for when it joins us we become familiar with it, at ease with it and, in essence, its humanity and our own are linked. In the world I mean – obviously not this or that world – everything is articulate. The way of meeting and parting pays homage to our humanity as such.

Concrete identity therefore is properly seen as a mechanical end-point. We know something as part of us when we understand its concrete identity. It not only has an identity but it has an identity for us. We in turn share our own identity with it and gain by it. Once I know who you are and understand what this means I can in truth call you my brother. Once the concrete identity of matter has been revealed to me I will know its use and understand its intrinsic purpose as real protection and security, for it is matter that is made manifest for us, not so that we scratch about in it and attempt to take it apart. So once we realize that matter is manifest we may rely on it for a while and we may relate to it most anywhere. We will also know perfectly well what not to expect from matter, such as the end of our extinction or the satisfaction of our desires or the rest we feel we have deserved, for these are transcendental, metaphysical and immaterial respectively.

The special individual as an exact momentum of growth signifies what it is, and its significance is understood as both spontaneous and dynamic.

For the intellectual appreciation of this an alternative category of progress is required so that we may limit our capacity for apprehension in favour of a quantitative increase of knowledge. Such an alternative category of progress may be obtained in the realm, or from the realm, of objects to which our study principally relates.

Objects relate to other objects with respect to our powers of observation: this really goes without saying. That our subject must at the same time relate to other subjects if we are not to indulge in exercises either empty or mischievous leads us to adopt various methods of inquiry and we remain alert to the definitively subjective origin of these methods especially while we propagate their application.

Subjective methods of inquiry into objective relationships encourage our powers of observation to remain suitable, so that we deal with objects within the context of their daily use.

This question, or notion, or the daily use of objects is of utmost importance. An object's content, therefore, is of interest to us beyond the incidental positioning during experiment. We maintain, therefore, that the interrelationship of objects entails their subtle surroundings, and equally, that during our observation of objects this entailment of their subtle surroundings is to be maintained.

An object is always surrounded by something else, which could, or might, in turn be dealt with as an object if we chose to do so. But of course we observe not so that we can say that we have observed, but because our observation has reasonable grounds and also a purpose in view.

We say that objects border on one another, and this has to do with their innate material make-up. In order to explain we might suppose that it should be impossible to differentiate between objects with the same material make-up, if indeed differentiation were what we had in mind.

While objects border on one another they cannot be said to have a border, since the border is comparative entirely. Only while we compare two or more objects, or sets of objects, does the concept of a border have any meaning. But while we observe the object or objects we wish to observe we become increasingly aware of a state of being inherent to each object or set of objects which tends to delimit, even in proportion to the intensity of our observational behaviour. It would not do to ignore this tendency or to belie its source; instead we strive to take it fully into account, only to observe how the same set of factors is then brought into operation with respect to that tendency itself. In short, what we soon realize is the missing link of ease. Only in ease can observation be honest, and only honest observation is of use. Its counterpart, when we strive to observe, for who knows what dishonest reason, is said to be diseased, and it is diseased observation which brings down, through abuse generally, the faculty of our senses to the level where they can only be described as animal at best or vegetal at worst.

Honest observation, then, is our goal and it proceeds in ease. The tendency in objects to assume fixed limits is due to a dishonesty in ourselves and therefore easily countered by an act of measurement.

Measurement counteracts the delimitation of objects. But we know from practice that measurement is part and parcel of the full act of observation, and so we understand that the delimitation of an object attests to an incomplete act of observation. As soon as measurement is stepped up, observation becomes full and our object is made reliable again. Technically we should not say 'again', because the reliable object has no capacity for delimitation nor can it be said to be susceptible to dishonest or diseased observation.

The easy, or honest, observation of reliable objects makes energy available. The energy it does make available however does remain objective. So we want to come to some conclusion as to the general application of objective energy and as to its particular worth. For we admit readily that energy in itself, considered often as no more than a by-product of activities pursued on a more or less massive scale, may mislead, due to its impulsive nature, and end by taking away from life rather than adding on to it. At the outset therefore we make a distinction between massive energy and energy that is lively. But this distinction has meaning and use as an expedient, in expediency, not itself objectively considered. We keep it in mind and apply it, in other words, as energy shows an inclination to become massive.

Lively energy articulates while massive energy pertains to itself. So much may be comprehended without stumbling into the trap of an illusory agreement between objects and things. The impertinence of massive energy has to be seen to be believed, and this defines the trap. Wisdom dictates the unbelievably of massive energy, i.e. that it deserves no credit, while everywhere we seem constrained to back up and confirm an uncertainty about it through the use of our senses. The truth of the matter lies the other way around. We are uncertain about massive energy due to a positive partial explanation through our senses, and with a total and thorough application of our senses the uncertainty should become complete. This is how the matter stands. Our senses serve us rightly in causing us to doubt the reality of massive energy. Extinct science tends to by-pass the senses so as to remove this doubt, in the vain hope that massive energy may become a utility, a product, a commodity, a concept of goods. Live science, the live science of mechanics, in our present case, teaches instead the fullest possible application of our senses in that very direction, so that the seeming reality of massive energy is unmasked and made totally obscure. Once made obscure, massive energy becomes inert and leaves no more traces, even, on our appreciation of reality. Massive energy appeals primarily to our sense of curiosity and tends to flatter our capacity for getting under our control mere potential. We se this control as a salutary admixture of preventative activity and perspicacity for the sake of man's performance in something that is popularly called nature, but the prevention can always be shown to be of that which is itself first called forth from the same point of view, while 'man's performance in nature' may be unveiled as a pose for the sake of false pride.

Our curiosity should instead be directed first and foremost towards itself, towards its own source in the intellect as ambition, and here it advocates a propensity for natural progress on the personal level, where we may take pleasure indeed in keeping under our control interminably the potential allotted to us at birth.

It makes no sense to speak of massive energy except insofar as we overcome it. The desire to make it serve may be understandable, but it should not be encouraged. An impatient nature deems it improbable that without some aspect of massive energy there can be ambition and success. But again, like curiosity, once ambition is scrutinized it reflects the inspiration of the age, while its adaptation to itself links it up to do combat against morbidity and joins it with an impulse of praise in the total eradication of negative matter. Success, consequently, pertains to the realm of derivative mechanisms and eventually it becomes situation quite happily within complexes of spontaneous drive.

Articulate energy has intelligent structure and is soundly felt. (Lively energy may be called articulate just as massive energy may be called impertinent, or honest observation easy.) By intelligent structure we mean the intelligently ponderable make-up of energy quanta and the perceptible exclusion by them of ineffective means.

Every impulse of articulate energy is momentarily attractive as strength and it directs as a technique. This allows us to observe such an impulse quite independently of a comparative system of reference, or of reference points.

The strength attraction of an articulate energy impulse makes us fit ourselves to it as we observe. We adapt, but not merely in order, but also in kind. This twofold adaptation energizes and brings about the collapse, in turn, of transient means, which would otherwise have attracted massive energy.

The technique direction of an articulate energy impulse makes us manipulate and manage a situation or a state of affairs to the point where minute energy quanta are relegated and held as consignments of operational energy; then these are suddenly released as effects, pure and simple, so that non-functional means are obviated, where otherwise, by their sheer presence, an analogue of massive energy would assume the position of structure, as a false structure.

The adaptation, the manipulation and management we mentioned, are part of what automatically happens as we observe reliable objects. They result, and we take full advantage of them. Our activity, we remember, is also passive. There is an energetic development which we aid and abet.

Take the sudden release of pure and simple effects, for example. Such effects have no calculable cause, and for this reason their production is traditionally aborted, when in fact they embody the peak performance of human intelligence and they alone remain. We therefore give ourselves wholly to such effects and permit their sustenance of our person. There can be no doubt as to the penetrability of them when it comes to alternate modes of experience, to exceptional circumstances physical or mental, to legitimate access phenomena, even, of regular interest only but profitable nevertheless when it comes to dealing with sets of fixed data or with static arrangements. We deal with these peripherally and in a sub-conscious manner. In other words we do not recognize them but we know they are there. We do not know them but we accept their existence. We do not deal with them in

69

person but vicariously. Legitimate access phenomena are epiphenomenal in character so that we look for nothing of benefit from them but we understand how and why they come to be. Access refers to the general introductory function of these phenomena insofar as they are sub-consciously conceived and not 'perceived or studied', which would not be possible in any case. Legitimate defines the institution of them as necessary and related to cause and effect in a necessary fashion.

The penetrability of pure and simple effects gives us opportunities for tendential growth, where we rely only on the ponderability of real bodies to facilitate our advance. In this way a real pleasure may be said to have us at its disposal, but more strictly speaking our experience is pleasure, rather than that we experience pleasure. The tendency to grow is then awareness of the fist order and effortless.

The intelligent structure of energy quanta affords us the special opportunity to align ourselves with gravitational forces in the interest of our comparison with those forces for the sake of emotional perfection.

We do all have an urge, even a compulsion, to perfect our emotions and the task is simplified if we persuade ourselves from the outset of the necessary and natural orderliness by which our emotions, viewed in themselves, desire to abide. The emotional aspect of sexual love, for example, one of the most difficult to reconstruct, correctly embodies electro-magnetic radiation which culminates forcefully, as force, in a personal transmission of love as such.

The embodiment of electro-magnetic radiation empowers our senses. We feel this radiation, so that material components of it preponder, to which we then give names, and whatever names are in justice available to us. Empty concepts are of no use. In the event of an accurate and decisive appraisal of the magnetic partiality which inheres in some particular object, there is an element of submission to the electricity flowing from one object to the other, and this facilitates the logical composure of our various faculties throughout the procedure. If, on the other hand, the electrical activity itself becomes objective for us, we do well to monitor and even license the characteristic ebb and flow of that activity, otherwise there will be distortion and waste. The tidal aspect of electromagnetic forces, and the cyclical character of whatever pertains to these forces, after the nature of an involvement, an entailment or an inclusion, appeals to our intellectual preference for repetitive experience and so our intellect likes to avail itself of ephemeral explications of this character and of the attributes that accompany it, but to no avail, or in vain, for eventually the will must break into that cycle and render it systematic. Gravitational forces are now liberated and annexed by the will so that they are given a territory for behaviour and a field of operation. Here begins the creative execution of all of our manly desires. Supervision of various initiatory anxieties should be encouraged. An express propagation of genial values usually proves itself of the essence, and this cannot be effectively disturbed or hindered by the critical reproach.

Creativity on account of gravitational force is certainly desirable, while its rejection on one count or another has caused us intensities of hardship. These intensities are meant to lead us back to the creativity we have spurned. We absorb their effects and elucidate the outcome of their sufferance.

But the creativity from gravitational force interjects sense where extension and continuity are interrupted. Extension and continuity may be usefully viewed as the two sides of size, and by recognizing the size of an object we extend our power over it and continue to possess it. The size of an object relates both to the size of other objects and to the power of recognition to which our subject has attained. An object is large or small, for example. According to the way in which we have learned to accommodate ourselves to that object's presence, and its presence retains for us an amount of intellect, a degree of sensitivity, a measure of per-

71

ception, and so on, and these help us to recognize the object in time, or after a time.

The recognized object is left in a constant state of familiarity and this is how we prefer to confront it while the various dimensions of our objectivity are still in the making. Dimensions here have to do with objectivity and not with objects themselves, whose lasting familiarity is soundly felt.

The dimensions of our objectivity depend directly and immediately on the intention of our subjectivity, and there is a beautiful consistency to be discovered in this, as a contemplative entity in itself or as an adaptable force of habit.

The subject intends, and this has value in itself. Were the subject to extend, it would be lost. The intending subject, therefore, may easily be directed in one way or another as long as the direction also has value. Misdirection is rejected because the subject is less intense. Not that the tension as such of the subject has any value. It merely registers, as a waning phenomenon, that misdirection is attempting to take place. An increase of tension, intentionally brought about, would be counterproductive.

The less intense subject may be redirected immediately, so that is intends, and then in one way or another.

But the intending subject does eventually arrive at the point where an object extends and now it goes into the make-up of that object. Objectivity as such is then recognized and encouraged to develop.

But we still have no object as such. For objectivity to end in an object requires dimension, and this is supplied on the spot as an act of expression. It does of course make good sense that this should be so, otherwise our best intentions would remain private obsessions, while the world would continue on its path, impracticable and as an idiocy.

The act of expression that brings the object, and with it the subject, of course, out into the open, so to speak, and into the light of day, is one of speech. In the presence of speech we are objectively viable. When we speak we extend the dimensions of our objectivity.

The object is whatever we make it, but finally it can only be the world. By the world we mean the world without end, not this or that world. This or that world is concluded and therefore remains excluded from us.

One of the uses of the science of mechanics is to keep this or that world separate from the world as such. Not that the world can be defiled, but the science of mechanics helps to prevent it from being defiled.

Here ends the science of mechanics.

***